That's unusual

Scripts from
Kath & Kim
Series 2

That's unusual

Scripts from *Kath & Kim* Series 2

Gina Riley & Jane Turner

ABC Books

Published by ABC Books for the
AUSTRALIAN BROADCASTING CORPORATION
GPO Box 9994, Sydney, NSW 2001

Copyright © Jane Turner & Gina Riley 2003

First published 2003

Copyright photography © ABC TV

All rights reserved. No part of this publication may be reproduced, stored in a retrieval system or transmitted in any form or by any means, electronic, mechanical, photocopying, recording or otherwise, without the prior written permission of the Australian Broadcasting Corporation.

ISBN 0 7333 1346 9

Designed by Ingo Voss, VossDesign
Colour separations by Colorwize Studio, Adelaide
Printed and bound by Griffin Press, Adelaide

5 4 3 2 1

Contents

1. The Announcement — 1
2. Inside Out — 36
3. The Moon — 67
4. Obsession — 98
5. My Boyfriend — 126
6. Another Announcement — 154
7. The Shower — 184
8. The Hideous Truth — 217

About Jane Turner and Gina Riley

Jane Turner is one of Australia's most popular comedians who is highly regarded for her writing, producing and performing in *Big Girl's Blouse* and *Something Stupid*, as well as her performances in *Fast Forward* and *Full Frontal*.

She is best known for her comic work, but she has also performed in a number of theatre productions *(The Rocky Horror Show, Popcorn, Man the Balloon)*, feature films *(Thank God He Met Lizzie)* and television dramas *(Prisoner, Cop Shop)*.

Gina Riley set out to become a serious dramatic actor, but was persuaded to attempt comedy by Glenn Robbins and Richard Stubbs. She started in stand-up and quickly moved into television comedy, appearing in *Fast Forward* and *Full Frontal* along with *Big Girl's Blouse* and *Something Stupid*, which she also wrote and produced.

Gina appeared in both series of *The Games* with John Clarke and Bryan Dawe, a role that combined her comic, dramatic and singing abilities. She sings the opening titles for *Kath & Kim*.

The Announcement

♠ Kim and Brett get back together
♠ Kath and Kel get counselling
♠ Kath and Kel nude up
♠ Sharon has her big date with Mark
♠ Kim falls pregnant

Scene 1 Interior – Restaurant – Night

Kim, Kath, Sharon and Kel are having dinner in a restaurant. It is New Year's Eve. Kim is shovelling in food, some of which she is taking from Kel's plate. Kath looks at her with distaste.

Kath
Oh!

Kim
What? Don't look at me like that, Mum. It's all you can eat.

Kath
Well do you think you can get your trotters out of the trough for five minutes, Kim? You're gross.

Kim
Oh, give it a bone, Mum. It's New Year's Eve.

Kath
Well I would give it a bone, Kim,
but you already ate it.

Kim eats some of Kel's sticky date pudding.

Kath
Hey! Don't have that. That's Kel's sticky date.

The Announcement

Kim
    Stuff youse then! I'll have Sharon's.

Kath
    No, Kim! Stop it!

Kim
    Yes!

Kath
    I'm not going to have you –

Kim
    Let go!

Kath
    – ruin –
    I'm not going to have you ruin our nice meal.

Kim sulks. Sharon gets a text message and laughs to herself.

Kim
    What are you laughing at, Sharon?

Sharon
    Oh, it's Mark. He's texted me again. Oh, I think he's really keen, Kim.

Kim
    Oh, if he's so keen, where is he tonight?

Kath
    What are you giving Sharon the third degree for, Kim? I think I'd be asking myself the same question, vis a vis, where is one Brett tonight?

Kim
    Rub it in, why don't you? It's not my fault that Brett won't speak to me and that he's changed the locks, and my marriage is up the proverbial.

Kath
    Shhh!

A good-looking waiter with a name tag 'Imran' comes over to take the plates.

The Announcement

Waiter
Hi, how were your meals?

Kath
Beautiful, Imran.

Sharon
Lovely, thanks.

Waiter
Great.

Waiter goes to take Kim's plate.

Kim
Oh! I'm still eating that.

Waiter
Sorry, I'll come back later.

Kath tries to engage the waiter in conversation.

Kath
Where are you from, Imran?

The waiter doesn't hear and leaves.

Kath
He didn't hear me.

Kim
Lucky him.

Kath
I'm just not surprised that Brett's had a gutful of your moods, Kim.

Kim
Pff!

Kath
Don't pff me, please. And it's ... I think it absolutely is your fault that you are once again spending NYE desperate and dateless.

Kim
For your information, Mum, I do have a date. A sticky date.

Kath
   Oh, don't be foul, Kim.

Kel dings his glass to make a speech.

Kel
   I'd like to, ah, say a few words.

Kath
   Oh.

Kel
   Tonight is Kath's and my's anniversary. One month, and they said it wouldn't last.

Kath
   Oh, Kel!

Kel
   I'd like to propose a toast to marriage, and to my spouse, Kath Day-Knight.

Kath
   Oh!

Kel
   I know that we haven't been able to be man and wife in the physical sense –

Kim
   People are eating!

Kel
   – but despite your osteoitis pubis and your temporarily foreshortened leg, you've made me a very happy man.

Kath
   Oh, thank you, Kel. And in reply, I would just like to say that yes, ah, since the accident at the wedding, it's true, I don't find my body as foxy as it once was, and my libido has gone AWOL.

Sharon
   Where?

Kath
> But I just want to say, Kel, you're only human, but you're the most patient damn human I know. So here's to you, Kel, and to my sexual urge. May it return with gusto before too long.

Kel
> To Kath's urge.

They toast.

Sharon
> To Mrs. D.'s urge.

Kim
> Yeah, I've got an urge. To throw up.

Kath
> Yes, well I have to say, your continued presence in the next-door bedroom is not helping one iota, Kim.

Kim
> Oh, right. So now it's my fault that you're a dried up old prude?

Kath
> I am not a dried up old prude, Kim. It's just that those paper thin walls, Kel's very shy about vocalising, that's all. Not that there's anything to vocalise about, but it's just one more spanner we've gotta deal with.

Sharon
> Oh my God, look at the time! It's nearly midnight! How about a nice bottle of French champagne?

Kim
> Ooh, yes!

Sharon
> My shout.

Kath
> Oh, have you got your wallet, Sharon?

The Announcement

Sharon
> Waiter! Can I have a bottle of your finest Don Paris Nong, thanks?

Waiter
> Sure.

Everyone
> Four, three, two, one ... Happy New Year!

Kath kisses Sharon with Kel, then Sharon kisses Kel, then her phone.

Kath
> Happy new year, Sharon.

Sharon
> Happy new year, Mrs. D. Happy new year, Kel. Happy new year, Mark!

Kel goes for the pash. Kath avoids and does a peck.

Kel
> Come here, you.

Kath
> Oh, happy new year. Kel.

Sharon
> Where's Kim gone, Mrs. D?

Kath
> Oh, I think she's in the toot, Sharon. I feel a bit mean now, poor Kim. I think she wants to avoid all this kissing hoopla.

Cut to Kim out near the toilet groping the waiter. They pash, then he tries to get away.

Kim
> Hey, I haven't finished yet!

She grabs another frightened waiter, but he evades her.

Kim
> Happy new year! Oh, your loss. I'm already taken. *(She shows her ring finger, but there are no rings.)* Happy new year!

Scene 2   Exterior – Kim and Brett's unit – Night

Kim stumbles up stairs and is banging on the door of her unit.

Kim
> Brett! Bretty!

We hear Cujo sniffing at the door.

Kim
> Oh, it's alright, Cujo. It's just Kimmy.

The dog starts barking madly. We hear Brett coming to the other side of the door. They talk through the door.

Brett
> Baa, Cujo. Get down.

Kim
> Brett, open the door.

Brett
> No, Kim. I can't see you right now.

Kim
> Oh please, Brett. I've just come 'round to say happy new year.

Brett
> No, Kim. It's over. I can't handle your moods.

Kim
> But I've changed.

Brett
> How?

Kim
> Well, not only am I super brown, but I've got a Killing Heidi hairdo.

Brett
> Oh! Oh, don't Kim. Don't tempt me.

Scene 3   Interior – Kath's house – Night

Kel puts on Kenny Loggins music and approaches Kath.

Kel
Can I tempt you, Kath, with a bit of ... Kenny Loggins? Come on. Let's do what we do best. Get the old team back together. Just like Bogan and Bacall.

Kath and Kel have an uncomfortable dance.

Kath
No, Kel, I'm sorry. Doll I can't boogie at this late stage. I might just sleep on the fold out again tonight.

Scene 4   Exterior – Kim and Brett's unit – Night

Kim
Bretty!

Brett
Go away, Kim. I'm trying to be strong.

Kim
Well, I'll change. I won't be moody.

Brett
How can I believe you?

Kim
'Cause I love you. I need you, and I'm busting. Brett please …

Brett slowly opens the door. Kim pushes past Brett.

Kim
And mind the corn rows.

Scene 5   Interior – Kath's house – Night

Kath is putting up the folding bed.

> **Kath** *(voiceover)*
> What the hell is wrong with you, Kath Day-Knight? You've got the world's biggest hunk-o'-spunk upstairs and you're down here on your Pat Malone. If I'm not careful, Kel's going to get a wandering eye. Actually, I think he did have a wandering eye before I met him. It's amazing, that laser surgery.

Scene 6   Interior/Exterior – Kath's house *(Backyard/kitchen)* – Day

The next day, Kath and Kel are having lunch alfresco.

> **Kel**
> Another oyster for the lovely lady?
>
> **Kath**
> No thanks, Kel. They make me gag.
>
> **Kel**
> How about another flute of bubbly?

She puts her hand over the glass.

> **Kath**
> No.
>
> **Kel**
> That windcheater's nice. Is it new?
>
> **Kath**
> Yes, I got it today. It came with its own pilling comb, which isn't a good sign.
>
> **Kel**
> I tell you what, those colourful parrots are doing things to me.

Kel tries to massage Kath's shoulders. She shrugs him off.

The Announcement

Kath
    Mind the shoulder pads, darl.

Kim and Brett arrive.

Kath
    Hello, you! Welcome back Cotter. Don't you look terrific, Brett!

Kim
    Oh, hello! What am I, chopped liver? Listen up, Mum. I've got good news.

Kath
    Oh, don't tell me. You and Brett are back together?

Kim
    How did you know? You're a psycho, Mum!

Brett
    Yep, me and Cujo decided to let her back in. We missed her mean little mug.

Kim
    Brett!

Kath
    Oh, well you know, I had a feeling in me waters! Oh, I'm that pleased. Here, give us a hug, Brett.

Brett
    Thanks, Mrs. D. I mean, Mrs. K.

Kath
    Oh, call me Kath.

Kim
    Thanks, Mum.

Kath
    Oh, it's terrific.

Kath hugs Brett. Kath hugs Kim. Kel and Brett shake hands. Kel goes to kiss Kim. She turns away.

Kim
    Anyway, I've just come to get my stuff.

The Announcement

Kath
(To Kel) Oh, isn't that good news? Kimmy's moving out of the next door bedroom.

Kel
Oh, I'm very excited.

Kel winks at Kath suggestively.

Kath
Oh, I don't mean that, Kel. I mean that it frees up that room for your bomber jackets and huge collection of man bags.

Kim
But wait, Mum. That's not the best news. Not only am I moving back into the marital unit, but Brett and me are going to –

Kath
Have a baby? Oh Kimmy, I had a hinkling, with the way you're eating.

Kim
No, Mum, we're going to try for a baby. I haven't fallen yet.

Kath
Oh well, that doesn't matter. It won't take you too long. You better get cracking, though, Kim.

Kim
Alright, Mum, I don't need you on my back as well as Brett!

Kath
Oh, okay, well I won't say another word. I'm just that thrilled!

Kim
I'm just going to go and get my stuff. Brett!

Brett
Okay.

Kath
Oh, isn't that exciting, Kel?

Kim
    Gotta catch me first.

Kel
    Kath, look at this. Get you going, does it?

Kath watches while Kel packs the plates into the dishwasher.

Kel
    Bit of a thinking man's foreplay. Stackin' the dishwasher.

Kath is unmoved.

Kath
    No. Nothing.

Scene 7   Exterior – Beach – Day

Brett and Kim are walking Cujo. Kim is eating an ice-cream. Brett is wearing really tight jeans.

Kim
    If I'm going to get pregnant, you're going to have to take those jeans off.

Brett
    What, here? Settle!

Kim
    Brett, they're too tight.

Kim
    And you can't wear jockettes. You'll have to wear boxers.

Brett
    There's nothing wrong with me, Kim.

Cujo goes for Kim's ice-cream.

Kim
    Oh, Cujo! Get down. No. No! Naughty girl! No!

Brett watches with a proud smile.

Brett
    You're gonna make a top mum, Kim.

The Announcement

Kim
I know.

Brett
Cuji girl. Cuji girl! Come here! Sit. You love your Bretty, don't you Cuji? Love your Bretty?

Cujo barks.

Brett
You love your Brett, Cuji? Love your Brett?

Cujo barks.

Brett
You love your Kim? You love your Kim, Cuji?

Cujo doesn't bark.

Kim
Cujo, you love Kimmy?

Cujo doesn't bark.

Kim
Stupid dog. We're getting rid of her once we have a baby. You know that, don't you Brett?

Scene 8   Interior – Kath's house *(Livingroom)* – Day

Kim is with Sharon and Kath.

Sharon
Wow! That is great news, Kim. So it hasn't actually happened yet?

Kim
No, but we're trying.

Sharon
Oh Kim, it's so exciting. Now Kim, what are you doing? Are you doing all the right things?

Kath
> Yes, how often are you and Brett having your relations? Are you going for it hammer and tong?

Kim
> You know your bee's wax, Mum? Why don't you mind it?

Kath
> And are you standing on your head for five minutes afterwards, Kim?

Kim
> Yes, Mum. I am not as stupid as I look.

Sharon
> Kim? Kim? Do you want a boy or a girl?

Kim
> Oh, a girl. Definitely.

Kath
> Well, you'll have to be creating an acidic environment for that, Kim. Are you using your vinegar?

Kim
> No, we ran out, so I used chutney.

Kath
> Oh, chutney.

Sharon
> Oh, nice.

Kim
> Yeah, nice.

Kath
> Nice. Yeah, that is nice.

Sharon
> Different.

Kim
> Yeah, different.

Sharon
> Unusual.

The Announcement

Sharon
No, no, Kim, I think it is lovely about you and Brett, because you're just such a good couple. And you know, Brett, he adores you, Kim.

Kath
He does.

Kim
Yeah, well, he's only human. I'm starving though.

Kim opens the fridge.

Kath
Hey Kim, get your nose out of my fridge, please. And leave off that Petit Miam.

Kim
Mum, it's a dairy snack. I need calcium if I'm to fall.

Kel enters. He has been for a run.

Kel
Hey, girls.

Sharon
Hi, Kel.

Kath
Hi, darl.

Kel
Hey, Kath.

Kel starts doing his stretches in the kitchen.

Kath
Oh, Kel, please.

Kel
Don't mind me. I'm just stretching me clacks.

Kath
You're a bit woofy, love.

Sharon's mobile rings. Sharon smiles as she checks another text message.

Kim
What's up with you, Sharon?

Sharon
Oh, it's Mark. He's asked me out on a proper date, to meet all his friends.

Kath
Oh, that's a very good sign, Sharon.

Sharon
Yeah, actually, he's invited me to a film buffs' party, and you have to dress as a film.

Kath
Oh, a film buffs' party. Well that sounds eye-brow!

Sharon
Yeah.

Kath
So what are you going to wear?

Sharon
Well, Mrs. D., my favourite film is, 'Dude, Where's My Car?' So, you know, I thought, I could go dressed as a dude.

Kath
Oh!

Kim
You'd be better off going as the car. Less make up. You know what my favourite film is? 'Shallow Hal'. I can relate.

Kath
Why? 'Cause you're big, Kim?

Kim
No, because I'm shallow. God, you're rude to me!

Kath
>Well, I like arty films. You know, 'Kundun', 'Bowling For Columbine', um, 'American Beauty'. Actually, Sharon, you could go as a plastic bag from 'American Beauty'! I've got a million of them in the pantry.

Kel
>My favourite film is 'Eyes Wide Shut'.

Kim
>'Eyes Wide Shut'? What's that?

Sharon
>Oh you know, Kim. It was Tom and Nicole's last film together.

Kath
>Yeah. 'Eyes Wide Shut'. Oh, that was a funny film. Actually, I might get that out on DVD. Yeah, get me out of myself. Anyway, I've gotta have a shower.

Kel
>Yeah. Yeah. So, haven't got a home to go to, Kim?

Kim
>Excuse me? Brett's at work, and I've come to do a load. Sharon, check my smalls, please. Sharon, my smalls!

Sharon
>Oh sorry, Kim.

Scene 9   Interior – Kath's house *(Upstairs bathroom)* – Day

Kel is knocking at the bathroom door where Kath is having a shower.

Kel
>Hey, sweets. How about you and I save some water?

Kath
>Oh, it's alright, Kel. I've put in a continuous hot water service.

Kel
> Oh, come on, Kath. Let me in. You're being silly.

Kath
> No, Kel. Use the other bathroom.

Scene 10   Interior – Fountain Gate Mall – Day

Sharon
> I don't think I will go dressed as a car, Kim. I just want to look really sexy for Mark. Can't think about it now. I'm starving. Can we go to the food court? This is really boring.

Kim
> Oh, in a minute, Sharon. Can you wait by Dumbo? I want to go into the chemist and get a pregnancy tester, alright?

Sharon
> Well how long are you gonna be? I want to go to the food court. I'm hungry.

Kim
> I said in a minute. If you ask again, you won't get a Yowie.

Sharon looks at Kim with pride.

Sharon
> Oh, you are gonna make a top mum, Kim.

Kim
> Wait.

Scene 11   Interior – Kath's house – Day

Kath is in her kitchen, taking Horny Goat Weed.

Kath *(voiceover)*
> Horny goat weed? Maybe this'll work. I'm feeling a bit of a goat at the moment.

Kim emerges with her pregnancy tester.

The Announcement

Kath
   Kim!

Kim
   Nuh. Negative.

Kim throws the pregnancy tester into the kitchen bin.

Sharon
   Hi, Kimmy.

Sharon enters wearing a homemade paper plate and tin foil mask and a cape.

Kim
   What have you come as, Sharon?

Sharon
   Oh, I took Kel's 'Eyes Wide Shut' idea. Remember the orgy scene with all the old men? Yeah, apparently it's really sexy. Do you think Mark will like it?

Kim
   No, it looks stupid. Anyway, I'm in crisis mode. It's not happening. Sharon?

Sharon
   Kim?

Kim
   I think I'm barren, Sharon.

Sharon
   Oh Kimmy, no.

Kim
   Stuff Mum. I'm gonna have a yoghurt.

Sharon
   Oh Kim, do you think you should? You know you're not meant – actually, they look really nice. Do you reckon I could have one?

Kim
   No, there's only two left.

Kim rushes from kitchen as car horn sounds.

Kim
    Oh, there's Brett. I'd better go. I'm ovulating.

Sharon takes off her costume, following Kim.

Sharon
    S'pose it is stupid.

Scene 12   Exterior – Brett's car – Day

Kim
    You took your time.

Brett
    Yeah, traffic was bad.

Kim is sulking in the passenger seat as Brett drives. Brett is wearing jeans with a paperbag-waist.

Kim
    Hurry up! You drive so slowly. You always stick to the speed limit. You're such a wuss.

Brett
    Don't call me a wuss, Kim.

Kim
    Well, you are a wuss. And why are you wearing those jeans?

Brett
    Well you told me to get rid of my tight stonewash. What's the matter with 'em?

Kim
    They've got a paperbag-waist and seams down the front. They're so girly.

Brett
    Yeah, well they're new.

Kim
    You should do something about that bald spot. It's getting bigger. Now let's get home quickly for once. We've gotta have sex.

Scene 13   Interior – Kath's house – Day

Kel closes sliding door.

> **Kel**
> Kath! I've got the 'Eyes Wide Shut' DVD and your scroggin!

He sees Sharon's costume on the counter. Kel smiles.

Scene 14   Interior – Kath's house – Night

Kath and Kel are finishing watching 'Eyes Wide Shut'.

> **Kath**
> Mmm! Not quite as funny as I remember.
>
> **Kel**
> Yeah. That, er, orgy scene was pretty raunchy, eh Kath? I'll see you upstairs?
>
> **Kath**
> Yeah, alright Kel.

Scene 15   Interior – Kath's house *(Bedroom)* – Night

Kath goes into the bedroom. Kel is in the costume sitting on the bed.

> **Kath**
> Kel! What are you doing?
>
> **Kel**
> Oh, you know, I found the costume lying around. I thought it was a hint. 'Eyes Wide Shut'.
>
> **Kath**
> Oh no, Kel. Oh, I think it's official, doll. My sex drive has left the building.
>
> **Kel**
> It's me, isn't it, Kath? You don't find me attractive anymore.

The Announcement

Kath
Oh, Kel, blind Freddy would find you enormously attractive. It's me. I mean, I can't see how you'd ever find me foxy again.

Kel pushes mask up onto forehead.

Kel
Ohh!

Kath
I mean, besides my hair, what else have I got going for me?

Kel
You'll do me any day, Kath Knight.

He goes to hug her. Kath stops him.

Kath
Oh, mind the wattle, Kel.

Kel
Look, we need help. Professional help. I think we need Marion.

Scene 16 Interior – Marion's house – Day

Kel and Kath on couch.

Kath
Don't know what we're doing here, Kel. It's very embarrassing.

Kel
What's so embarrassing about a couple of baby boomers who can't get their rocks off?

Kath
What can she tell me about connubial sexuality? I mean, look at her. She looks like a nun!

Kel
Shh!

Kath
　　Don't shoosh me, please.

Marion
　　Okay, well ... Kel has told me all about your little problem, and the good news is, that it is easily fixed. Okay? I'm going to show you some cards now.

Marion holds up inkblot card.

Marion
　　And I want you to tell me what you see.

Kel
　　A couple making love.

Marion nods.

Kath
　　Two dead sticks.

Marion
　　And this one? What do you see here?

Kel
　　A man and a woman locked in a passionate embrace.

Kath
　　A wettex and a squeedgee.

Marion
　　Okay, good. Let's try another approach.

Scene 17　Interior – Computacity – Day

At Computacity there is a queue of customers. Brett is on the phone to Kim.

Brett
　　Yes, you're a hornbag. *(To customer)* Sorry, didn't mean you. I mean, yes, you are a hornbag. *(Into phone)* What? Your eggs? Kim, I can't talk now. I got customers. Yeah, I'm sure your biological clock'll still be ticking by the time I get home.

Scene 18   Interior – Kath's house – Day

Kim is on the telephone, and taking her temperature. She has a thermometer in her mouth. She takes it out and picks up a cigarette.

Kim
It doesn't tick, Brett. It's digital. Well, you'll just have to leave work early. Well grow a brain, Brett. I can't do this on my own. No, I'm at Mum's. Now!

Scene 19   Interior – Marion's house – Day

Kath and Kel are wearing blindfolds. Kel rubs hands over jacket.

Marion
And get in touch with your body. And, blindfolds off.

Kath and Kel take off their blindfolds to see Marion in the nude.

Kath
Oh! Marion, your kimono seems to have come loose.

Marion
It's all part of the therapy. Mine, not yours.

Kel
Oh. Really?

Marion
But it's given me a brilliant idea. Let's have a pow wow. Anyone for Jarrah?

Kel
I'll give you a hand with the mugs if you like, Marion.

The Announcement

Scene 20 Exterior – Car parked at supermarket – Day

Kath and Kel are going for it in the car. We hear the song 'Insatiable'.

Kath
Oh, I think I'm back, and big time!

Kel has beaded seat covers, like a taxi driver.

Kel
Oh, I think I need some sheepskin car seat covers, sweets.

Scene 21 Interior – Kath's house – Day

Kim and Brett are coming down the hall from upstairs.

Brett
Oh come on, Kim. Kel's man bags put me off.

Kim
Oh, thanks for nothing, Brett. At the rate we're going, it's never going to happen.

Kath enters through the backdoor, completely naked but carrying some discreetly positioned bags of groceries.

Kath
Oh, hi Kim!

Kim
Mum, what are you doing?

Kath
I've just been shopping. What does it look like? Come and give me a hand.

Kath
Hi, Brett. Ooh, I like that tie.

Kel comes in. He is also naked.

Kel
Gidday, folks. Give us a hand, will you Brett? Thanks.

Kim
>   Mum! Put some clothes on. It's revolting!

Kath
>   No Kim, it's beautiful.

Kim
>   Not from where I'm sitting.

Kath
>   Now are you two love birds staying for tea? I'm doing bangers and mash.

Kim
>   Oh, I feel sick.

Kath
>   Oh, I could be offended by that, Kim, but I won't be because I'm feeling too damn good about myself. How's work, Brett?

Brett
>   Oh yeah, good, Kath.

Kath
>   Yeah? How are sales?

Brett
>   Yeah, great. Yeah, look, I gotta go back to work. Kim, I'll give you a lift if you like.

Kath
>   Oh, alright. I do like that tie.

Kim
>   Yep, yep, yep, yep.

Kel
>   Where do you want these onions, doll?

Kath
>   Ah, in the pantry cupboard, right in the corner. You gotta bend right over to get in there, Kel. Right over.

Kim and Brett look at Kel bending over. Their faces register horror.

The Announcement

Scene 22   Exterior – Kath's house – Day

Kath and Kel are out the front, gardening. Kath waves to a startled neighbour.

Kath
> Hello! Yes, it's only natural, you know. We've all got one. Take a photo. It'll last longer. Hi, Sharon.

Sharon
> Hi, Mrs. D. Kel.

Kel
> Sharon.

Sharon
> What's all this?

Kel
> Kath's in therapy, Sharon. Marion feels that Kath is hiding from her problems.

Kath
> Yes, Sharon. And she feels that the more light I can shed on them, the better I'll feel within myself.

Kel
> Oh, you feel alright to me, foxy.

Kath
> Oh, right back at ya, mister!

Sharon
> Wow, that's great, Mrs. D.

Kath
> Yes, it is Sharon, but it's very strict. You know, I'm not allowed to shut my body up in tops or slacks, but I have got special dispensation to wear my gumnut earrings and a bum bag when shopping.

Kel
> Oh, that Marion is a genius.

Kath
> Yes.

Kel
> Listen, I might pop inside and get on the exercise bike and do a few Ks.

Kath
> Alright, you great hunk-o'-spunk. Sharon, it's your big party tonight, isn't it?

Sharon
> Oh, yeah. I'm so excited, Mrs. D. I still haven't got a costume to wear yet, though. I really want to look nice for Mark and his friends. Mrs. D., what do you think really impresses guys?

Kath
> Well, Sharon, I think Doctor Sigmund Freud said it best when he said guys love ladies in the nude.

Sharon
> Nude?

Kath
> Mm.

Sharon
> Well, it is a film buffs' party. Oh! Thanks, Mrs. D!

Kath
> That's alright, Sharon. Have a great time tonight and fingers and toes with Mark, love.

Sharon
> Alright!

Kel
> Oh! Kath!

Kath
> Kel?

Kel
> Quick!

Kath
> Kel?

Scene 23 Interior – Kath's house – Day

Kath runs in to see Kel naked on the floor with the exercise bike on top of him.

> **Kel**
> Oh Kath, quick! Oh!
>
> **Kath**
> Ohh! Kel!
>
> **Kel**
> Ohhh!
>
> **Kath**
> Kel! Are you alright?
>
> **Kel**
> Ohhh!
>
> **Kath**
> Ohh! I'll get the wheat bag and put it in the microwave. Stay there.

Scene 24 Interior – Kath's house – Day

> **Kath**
> Take the ice pack off it, Kel! I'll be back up in a moment with your yoghurt and muesli.

Kim goes into the bathroom and checks her Predictor pregnancy tester, which is sitting on the bench.

> **Kim**
> Oh come on!
>
> **Kim** *(voiceover)*
> There must be something wrong with Brett. Why isn't it happening? It couldn't be my fault. I mean, look at me. I'm young. Well, I don't look my age, that's for sure.

Kim enters kitchen and throws test in bin.

Kim
> Negative.

Kath in kitchen spoons out muesli. Sharon opens sliding door wearing neck brace.

Kath
> Oh, hi, Sharon. How was your big date?

Sharon
> Not so ace actually, Mrs. D.

Kim
> What happened?

Sharon
> Well, I took your advice re the costume –

Kath
> Yeah.

Sharon
> – or lack of, and it was all going really great until we had to play blind man's bluff. And when it was my turn to wear the blindfold, I tripped over and went A over T in the middle of the circle. And after that, Mark said that he thought we were seeing too much of each other. Well, he felt that he'd seen enough of me for the time being.

Kath
> Oh, he got a bit of a rude shock, did he, Sharon?

Sharon
> There are many things that a first date can survive, Mrs. D., but falling over awkwardly, in the nuddy, is not one of them.

Kath
> Ho! Tell me all about it. Just when I am back to my flagrant self, Kel's gone and lost his why-nor-where-for.

Sharon
> Anyway, doesn't matter.

Sharon is depressed.

The Announcement

Kath
Oh, Sharon. *(Whispers)* Kim! Say something!

Kim
Sharon? You can have my Petit Miam if you like. I do not need the calcium. Obviously I'm barren.

Sharon
Really? Oh Kimmy, I'd love that.

Kath
Anyway girls, I tell you, I am so up for it since my therapy finished, I might have to go and pop myself on St. John's Wort if I'm not careful.

Kim
Mum!

Kath
Kimmy, would you smoke outside, please?

Kim
No. I'm depressed.

Kath
Kim, Kel doesn't know I'm still smoking. I've told him I've given up. Outside!

Sharon
Kim! Your pregnancy tester. It's not negative. Two lines means positive.

Kath
Ohh!

Kim
What, you're kidding? Wh – I've been pregnant all this time? You mean I've been having sex with Brett for no good reason?

Kath
Oh!

Sharon
Kim! You are gonna have a baby!

Kim, Sharon and Kath scream.

Kath
Oh my God, that means I'm gonna be a nana. Oh, I can't be a nana! I'm too young! Get on the blower! Get on the blower, Kim, and call Brett!

Kim
Oh, keep your wig on! Oh my God.

Kath
What's the matter, Kim? It is Brett's, isn't it?

Kim
Yes, of course it's Brett's.

Sharon
How about I crack open the Tia Maria and put on the footy franks.

Kim
Oh don't, Sharon. Oh! No, that's it. I'm going to have to quit work. I feel so sick.

Kath
Oh Kimmy, Kimmy, Kimmy. Look at me, look at me, look at me, please. Now I've got one word to say to you. Morning sickness, reflux, unbearable agony, stitches and after all that, shocking incontinence.

Brett enters in the nude. They all look.

Sharon
Brett!

Kim
Brett!

Kath
Hello, Christmas.

Brett
I think I've found the answer to our problems, Kim.

Kim
Oh, as per usual, your timing's way out.

The Announcement

Kim holds up pregnancy test.

Kim
    The test is positive.

Brett
    Oh, Kim!

Brett goes to hug Kim.

Kim
    No, don't.

Kath
    Let me be the first to congratulate you, Brett. Congratulations.

Sharon
    I'm so happy. You guys are back together again, and you're having a baby, and Mrs. D., you've got your urge back!

Kath
    Yes!

Sharon starts crying.

Sharon
    And I've got no one!

Kim
    Could you all stop crying?
    Now if there's one thing I can't bloody stand, it's crying!

Kath looks at Kim proudly.

Kath
    You're gonna make a beautiful Mum, Kim!

Kim
    I am.

Scene 25 Exterior – Kath's house – Day

Kath and Kim sit out in the backyard.

Kim
God, she looks terrible!

Kath
Who?

Kim
She should have some work.

Kath
Nick Nolte?

Kim
Yeah.

Kath
Mm.

Kim
Oh, I'd kill for a wine.

Kath
Have one. I drank like a fish when I was pregnant with you. We all did. And look at you, you're – actually, you'd better not.

Kim
I've gotta say, my morning sickness nicked off once you put your clothes back on.

Kath
Very funny, Kim. No, I now realise how damn good my body is.

Kim
Oh, you look like Lady Cadaver.

Kath
Thank you, Kim. I take that as a compliment. No, but I have to say, I don't know how long, Kim, I would have lasted without my accessories.

Kim
This dip tastes like metal.

Kath
Mm, get used to it. No, I did feel terribly free walking around nude, but you know me. I was bored. I like to team with the theme. You know, designing my accessories, that's my life.

Kim
Hey Mum?

Kath
Mm?

Kim
Does it hurt?

Kath
What, being a nudist? Yes, it does sometimes.

Kim
No, childbirth.

Kath
Oh no, not at all

Inside Out

- Kim and Brett renovate their apartment
- Kath resents Kel doing too much around the house
- Sharon plays war games

Scene 1   Interior – Kath's house – Night

Sharon and Kath are watching football on the telly.

Kath
> Go, go! Come on, Tigers! Oh, come on, pick it up, you pack of girls! Oh, umpire, you white maggot! Read the rule books!

Sharon
> Go Cambo!

Kath
> Go, Ritcho. You got it now. Come on, kick it, kick it, kick it! Look at the time!

Final siren goes.

Kath
> Oh, hopeless. Bum! Forty one points. Hopeless, Tigers. Oh, it's humiliating.

Sharon
> Gonna have to do better against the Swans next week, Mrs. D.

Kath
> Oh, it's depressing, Sharon. I s'pose it's only the pre-season. Doesn't really matter. Anyway, change the subject. What are you up to for the long weekend?

Kath puts on a glove then picks up cigarette.

Sharon
> I got war games on, Mrs. D.

Kath
> Mmm, war games? What does that pacifically entail, love?

Sharon
> Dressing up as soldiers and fighting each other in the bush.

Kath
> Mm.

Sharon
> Yeah. Need to know basis. Can't say too much, but, um, it's at Daylesford this year.

Kath
> Daylesford? Oh, that's nice, isn't it Sharon? Because once you've been killed, you can go shopping.

Sharon
> What about you? What are you up to?

Kath
> Oh, up to pussy's bow. I tell you Sharon, this marriage caper's really got me on the hop. Like for instance, Saturday night, I'm going to do a huge slap up meal for Kel. Because you know how much he likes my chicken feet.

Sharon
> Oh, who doesn't, Mrs. D?

Kath
> Yeah, well I've got Donna Hay's newy and so I'm going to do the Chinee degustations menu. It looks to die for. Oh quick, it's back on, Sharon. Unmute the button.

Kim enters livingroom through sliding door and walks past Sharon to Kath in kitchen.

Kath
Kim. What are you doing back? God, haven't you got a home to go to?

Kim
Turn the telly off, Sharon.

Kath
No –

Kim
I've got big news.

Kath
Kim, I'm watching that!

Kim
No, this is important. You're going to die, Sharon.

Sharon
Me? Why?

Kath
What's happened, Kim? Don't tell me! You're having twins. I knew it!

Kim
No, no, better than that.

Kath and Sharon
What?

Kim
Well tonight, Brett picked up on the fact that I was in a foul mood, which as you know is not like me. We were watching 'Changing Rooms', when he came out of the blue and said it.

Kath and Sharon
What?

Kim
What I've been waiting to hear for a long time.

Kath
>No!

Kim
>Yes, the R word. Yes, we're renovating.

Kath
>Kimmy!

Sharon
>Oh, Kimmy, Kimmy, oh my God!

Kath
>So pleased.

Sharon
>Not only are you and Brett together again, but you're having a baby and you're going to have renovations as well!

Kath
>That'll be so good for your marriage.

Kim
>I know. I told Brett the only way our marriage will survive is if we renovate and live in the renovations while we do them ourselves.

Kath
>Yes, very wise. Good girl.

Kim
>Yes.

Kath
>Oh, and what an adventure. It is so exciting, when you still haven't finished your renovations and your baby arrives early.

Kim
>Oh, I know. It's going to be so good for us. So exciting.

Sharon
>Oh, this calls for Barbecue Shapes and a bottle of Bailey's.

Kath
> Yes! So much fun!

Kim
> So much to do, I can't believe it.

Kath
> Yes, Kimmy, 'cause we better put our thinking caps on. I mean, what style are you thinking of? I mean, Sante Fe or period?

Kim
> Well, I'm thinking period because it's an old unit, built last century, 1998.

Kath
> Yeah, but period's fiddly, love. And look, I don't think I can help you at the moment, now that I'm married. I mean, come on.

Kim
> No Mum, it's alright. Brett and I are going to do it ourselves. He's taking time off work. But Sharon ...

Sharon
> Kim?

Kim
> 'Cause you're my second best friend, will you come and do the heavy lifting for me tomorrow?

Sharon
> I can't, Kim. I've got war games on this weekend.

Kim is not happy.

Sharon
> But I'll bring you back something really great from Daylesford for the reno.

Kim
> Well, if it's for the nursery. I'm doing it all Mambo.

Kath
> Oh Kimmy, your nursery? How cute!

Kim
    I know, I know. It's going to be so good. I've got it all sussed. I'm going to put a freeze all around –

Kath
    Oh no, no, not a freeze. You should existential the walls. I mean, I could help you with that if I had more time, because of course, I've done the TAFE course.

Kim
    Oh Sharon, come and have a look at my *Inside Out*.

Sharon
    Oh, really?

Kim
    It's got some great ideas.

Kath
    Yeah.

Kim
    For the nursery.

Kath
    Oh, God, look at the time! Oh, I've got to go and put those recycle bins back in the bay ...'cause Kel's going to come and park the Daiwoo. And I've got to microwave the lasagne and ...

Kim
    ... you'll see, I want to pick up that colour ...

Kath
    Oh bum, I forgot to pick up Kel's scotch guarded bomber from the bloody dry cleaners! Too much to do!

Kel enters carrying a scotch-guarded bomber jacket and a lasagne.

Kel
    Hi, sweets. One scotch guarded bomber, one piping hot lasagne and the recycle bins are back in the bin bay.

Kath
> Oh, well you're not just a pretty face, are you? So how do you want to do it? Do you want to have tea first, or would you like to have some wine and nibblies to start?

Kel
> Let's have a drink. I need to debrief.

Kath
> Do you, mister? Well, I like what I hear.

Kel
> Uh-uh, you sit down. I'll get it.

Kath
> No Kel, I can get it. You've been working.

Kel
> Come on, come on.

Kath
> Kel, you're tired.

Kel
> Sit.

Kath
> Oh, Kel. Well I could get very used to this. Yes. Very used to it.

Kath sits down. Kel brings over the glass of wine and two coasters.

Kel
> Uh-uh.

Kel
> Lift up.

Scene 2   Interior – Kim and Brett's unit – Day

Kim and Brett are in the flat. They are wearing matching shirts like the show 'Changing Rooms'.

Brett
> Yeah. I thought we'd do the bathroom shabby chic, Kim.

Kim
> There's aluminium windows in there. It's got to be in keeping. It's got to be Victorian.

Brett
> No way!

Kim
> Way, Brett. Cujo!

Brett
> Alright. So, are we going to rag the walls in the hall?

Kim
> We'll see. Right, I really want eggplant in here. It's going to be so nice.

Brett
> Oh, nah. Yuck.

Kim
> Brett, if we're going to renovate, it's gotta be give and take, you know.

Brett
> Yeah, I give, you take.

Kim
> Excuse me?

Brett
> Well we're not having eggplant in here. It's too girly, that's final.

Kim
> Oh, I can't believe you, Brett.

Brett
> Kim.

Kim
> I just want eggplant in the vestibule. Is that too much to ask?

Brett
> Yeah, alright.

Kim
> And the hot pink poofs as well.

Scene 3   Interior – Kath's house – Day

Kel is in the spare room putting all the winter clothes in a vacuum-sealed bag.

Kath
> Kel, doll? Kel? Have you seen my Coogi cardigan? The one with the batwing sleeves?

Kel
> I've got it here. I'm vac-packing it. I'm putting all the spare jumpers into storage.

Kath
> But I'll be cold, Kel.

Kel
> Put on a long sleeve blouse or something.

Kath
> *(Sotto voce)* Can you not leave your wet towel on the bed, please. Right, what have I got to do? *(To Kel)* Kel, I might give these drawers a bit of a birthday.

Kath opens a drawer. All her underwear is ironed and folded meticulously.

Kel
> Oh, been there, done that. Hope you don't mind. I had the iron on so I gave your bras a bit of a press as well.

Kath
> Oh, you're unbelievable, Kel! Alright, well tonight's tea's done. So I might get cracking on tomorrow night's tea.

Kel
> Tomorrow night's tea's under control, Kath!

Scene 4 Interior – Kim and Brett's unit – Day

Brett and Kim are fighting over the livingroom furniture.

Kim
   No, that's my final word on that, Brett. Oh and another thing, that table's gotta go.

Brett
   Hey? That's grandma's. This is antique cedar. It's a beautiful piece of timber. It's worth eight grand.

Kim
   Oh, in your dreams! It's revolting. It's old and stained.

Brett
   It's staying, Kim.

Kim
   Well look at my chairs. They're distressed. They don't go with it.

Brett
   It's staying, Kim. Bad luck.

Kim
   I hate you, Brett.

Scene 5 Interior – Kath's house – Day

Kath has the cookbook out. She is making cold rolls.

Kel
   Careful. That rice paper is very delicate, okay? You'll need to put a damp cloth over those.

Kath
   Yes, alright, Kel. God, who do you think you are? Geoff Jansz? I wish. And could you get out of my kitchen please, Kel?

Kel
   Uh-uh-uh, our kitchen.

Kath
   Ah, what have you done with my Rove Live mug, too?

Kel
   All the mugs are now up top.

Kath
   But I can't reach them up there, Kel.

Kel
   It'll do you good to stretch.

Kath
   And what about the utensils that were in it?

Kel
   Ah, in the second drawer, in alphabetical order. Please don't go muckin' 'em up, alright?

Kath
   Alright.

Kel goes to the stove and turns all the handles in.

Kel
   Handles in, thanks sweets. Uh uh, that's what the spoon rest is for. And that needs a little extra salt, okay? Terrific.

Scene 6   Interior – Brett and Kim's unit – Day

In the livingroom, Kim is casually putting the final touches on the cedar table. She has painted the antique table distressed blue. Brett sees.

Brett
   What are you doing? Stop! Oh Jesus Christ!

Kim
   No, I think it looks really nice. Looks really old now. I sandpapered off that French polish. It's period now. I thought we agreed we were going to renovate period style.

Brett
   Oh, I gotta get out of here.

Kim
> What?

Brett
> I can't talk to you now, Kim.

Kim
> What?

Brett
> I'm bloody angry.

Brett storms out of the room. Kim follows and sees Brett's handiwork.

Kim
> Brett!

Brett
> What?

Kim
> What have you done to my vestibule? It's yellow and white.

Brett
> Yeah, egg plant. Yellow and white.

Kim
> Not egg, eggplant. Eggplant is purple, you fool! I'm pregnant! I don't need the stress! I'm bloody gropable, Brett!

Scene 7   Interior – Kath's house – Day

Kath *(on phone)*
> Oh Kim, calm down. It's just your marriage. More importantly, for Kel's tea tonight, I've done the Donna Hay. You know the Chinese banquet? Yeah. So look, I'm frantic. I gotta go. Yeah, I gotta go, Kim. I've gotta unload the dishwasher. Alright, see ya. Bye.

Kath hangs up then opens the door to the dishwasher to find it empty.

Kath
> Oh. Super Kel strikes again. *(Voiceover)* Right, nine am. House is clean. Tea's done. There was something I was going to do today. Alright, I'd better get cracking on some of those important projects of mine.

We see Kath peeling stickers from the apples. Kath moves to different rooms of the house doing absolutely nothing. Kath calls Kel.

Kath
> Hi, Kel. Yeah, it's only me. Busy? Oh, yeah, flat out. Yeah. Had your morning tea? What'd you have? Oh no, sorry love, yeah. I've gotta go too. Yeah, okay. Alright. Oh, Kel, what time'll you be home? Yeah, okay doll. And don't forget tea tonight, Kel …

Scene 8   Interior – Kel's butcher shop – Day

Kel hangs up from Kath too early. Kel talks to a customer.

Kel
> … sorry Mrs. Ellis. That was Kath. I'm doing surprise chef for her tonight. She's gonna flip.

Woman
> Oh, sounds lovely. Bye, Kel.

Kel
> See ya. Okay Tony, be back in about half an hour.

Tony
> Yeah, righto, Kel!

Scene 9   Interior – Brett and Kim's unit – Day

Kim puts some items in the bin, including a framed photo of Cujo.

Brett
> Cuji girl. Come here!

Scene 10 Interior – Kath's house – Day

Kath hangs around with nothing to do.

> **Kath (voiceover)**
> What is the time? Eleven thirty. Yeah, I might pop down to IKEA. Will I go now? What have I got on tomorrow? Nothing. I better go now.

Scene 11 Interior/Exterior – Car/Nepean Highway – Day

> **Kath**
> Oh, what am I doing? I don't really want to go to IKEA.

Kath turns car around and heads back.

> **Kath**
> Maybe I should go.
> Oh no, won't bother. I know, I'll go and see Kim.

Scene 12 Interior – Brett and Kim's unit – Day

> **Brett**
> Come on, Kim. Please open the door.
>
> **Kim**
> Oh, I'm not talking to you. I want a divorce!
>
> **Brett**
> I'm so sorry. If it means that much to you, look, we can keep the Bumbalina.
>
> **Kim**
> If I'd known you didn't like Bumbalinas I never would have married you.
>
> **Brett**
> Oh come on, Kim. Look, where do you want me to put it?
>
> **Kim**
> You can stick your Bumbalina right up your –

Kath
> Hello, peoples! It's only me. Oh, yes. Yes. I am liking this eggplant. Gee, rest of the place is a bit of a shambles isn't it? God, lucky I'm here.

Scene 13 Interior – Homewares shop – Day

Kel wanders into the homewares shop. Prue and Trude are behind the counter talking.

Prue
> You look tired, Trude.

Trude
> Well, I'm doing it tough at the moment, Prue. You know, Graham's never home. He's up to his ears in boobs at the moment.

Prue
> Well I guess that's what you get for being married to Melbourne's most successful plastic surgeon.

Trude
> Yes, you're right. You going away for the school holidays?

Prue
> Oh look, we were going to go to Falls, but there's no snow.

Trude
> No?

Prue
> No, so yeah. I don't know. What about you?

Trude
> I just want to go bush, you know. Somewhere off the beaten track.

Prue
> Really? So where're you going to go?

Trude
> Noosa.

Prue
>Oh, great. Yeah, we went there last year. Adrian had a psych conference. I had to entertain all the visiting fellows.

Trude
>At the conference?

Prue
>Oh no, in bars, my room. You know, wherever.

Trude
>Oh, great!

Prue
>Oh God, Trude. Look at the matching shoes and jacket.

Trude
>It's a vision in vinyl.

Prue
>Hello! How are you?

Kel
>Oh, no complaints.

Prue
>Oh, God, I'd better go and help this woman with the ruched cargo pants. I mean, what has she come as?

Trude
>Hi, now can we help you, or are you just happy browsing?

Kel
>I'm looking for a fish kettle. I'm doing cod on the hot rocks for my wife tonight.

Trude
>Mm. Special occasion?

Kel
>Oh, no. I always like to cook for my lady.

Trude
>Oh. Prue!

Prue
>Yeah?

Trude
> You've gotta hear this. This guy's cooking for his wife.

Prue
> Oh, really? Well I'd love to meet the lucky lady who snared you.

Kel
> She's pretty special.

Prue
> Oh, I'm darn sure she is.

Trude
> Well I think you're great. You know, my husband Graham is useless in the kitchen.

Prue
> Yeah, but great in the sack.

Trude
> Oh Prue, you're a scream.

Prue
> Oh what? We've been on for years, you know that. Having a raging affair.

Trude
> Is that why you always look like the cat who swallowed the King Island double cream?

Prue
> Oh, stop, stop! You're dreadful. You're dreadful, Trude. No, he is. He always comes up with the goods. Always comes up trumps. You know, he's like John Major. Big in his underpants.

Trude
> Oh, you must be thinking of another Graham, not mine.

Kel
> My, ah, fish kettle?

Trude
> Oh, it's down the back.

Prue
    Yeah, they're all there.

Prue
    Pie Lavet, Le Creuset.

Trude
    Oh Prue, did I tell you? I did a beautiful cassoulet in my Le Creuset yesterday.

Prue
    Oh really? *(Answers phone)* Hello? No, I'll have to put you on hold, I'm sorry. Well I spilt my latte on my duvet.

Trude
    Oh, did you pop it in the Miele?

Prue
    No. *(Into phone)* Hello? No.

Trude
    What can I do now?

Prue
    (Into phone) Haven't got any of those.

Trude
    Nothing?

Prue
    No.

Scene 14 Interior – Brett and Kim's unit – Day

Kath is speed-reading a document with Brett looking on.

Kath
    No, no, you don't have to go to Council over that. A neighbour's tree, it's not a town planning issue.

Brett
    Do you think we'll get into trouble?

Kath
> Well just don't tell them. I mean, just take their bloody tree out. You're entitled to light.

Brett
> Yeah. Looks pretty old.

Kath
> Oh, all the more reason to get rid of it. I mean, the next storm it could blow over and come crashing down on your new tiles.

Kim
> The neighbours'll go ape, Mum.

Brett
> No, no, your Mum's right, Kim. If we don't act now, it could be a disaster.

Kim
> Alright, don't listen to me then.

Brett
> Well don't get pussy bum, Kim.

Kim
> No, thank you, Brett. You can get stuffed, the pair of you.

Kim storms out.

Kath
> Oh, what'd I say? I'm the ogre today.

Brett
> No, that's Kim. And her hormones.

Kath
> Oh Brett, you're too nice. Look, how about I take her for a bit of a drive down the Golden Mile? We'll suss out some fittings and such. Leave you in peace to silly putty your cornices?

Brett
> Thanks, Mrs. D.

Kath
> Kimberly!

Brett
> Kath.

Kath
> Thank you.

Scene 15 Interior/Exterior – Car/Nepean Highway –Day

Kath is parking.

Kim
> What are you doing? Why are you parking here? There's parking over there.

Kath
> Yeah, but I don't want to have to pay, Kim.

Kim
> No it's for free.

Kath
> I don't care. They say that, but then you get your fine in the mail for a hundred bucks. Haven't you seen 'Enemy Of The State', Kim? Cameras all around.

We see Kath and Kim crossing the busy highway.

Kath
> Oh, no.

Kim
> What?

Kath
> Oh, that's embarrassing. I've been walking around all day with my seam not straight.

Kim
> Oh Mum, get a life.

Kath
> Don't say that, Kim. I have got a life.

Kim

    Anyway, back to me. I have got the concept for the kitchen. Very exciting.

Kath

    Oh well, you'd better tell me, Kim, 'cause I need to approve it, so shoot.

Kim

    Alright, Brett and me have decided we want solid monogamy.

Kath

    Oh no, Kim, monogamy's very old fashioned. You just need a veneer of monogamy. That's all people care about.

Kim

    Oh, here we are.

Kath

    No, I want to go to Handles Plus.

Kim

    No, I want to go to Knobs and Knockers. I know what I want, Mum.

Kath

    No you don't, Kim. Come with me. I need to get you sorted.

Kim

    Oh look, Mum. There was a park right out the front.

Kath

    Alright. I still maintain my park was better.

Scene 16   Interior – Kim's and Brett unit – Day

Kim

    Yep.

Kath

    No. No, Kim. Brett, put it back here in the middle of the room please.

Kim
    No Mum. There'll be no room for anything else.

Kath
    No, it's good right there –

Kim
    Put it against the wall, Brett.

Kath
    No, Brett, here in the middle of the room –

Kim
    Mum, will you please butt out –

Kath
    It's much better –

Kim
    We've got to live   what do you know about ...

Kath
    Now Brett ...

Kim
    Oh, alright then. I won't do anything.

Kim sulks.

Kath
    Kimmy. Kimmy, look at me, please. Look at me. Look at me. Now I've got one word to say to you, Kim. Feng Shui.

Kim
    What?

Kath
    Well if you put your desk against the wall, you've got your back to the door, so your enemies can come in at any time and clock you on the head.

Kim
    Someone's gonna clock you on the head in a minute.

Kath
    What's that, Kim?

Kim
>Nothing. Just said we need a clock by the bed.

Kath
>Oh yes, I heard. Alright. Well I'll be in the kitchen then.

Scene 17 Interior – Kath's house – Day

Kel is in the kitchen. Kel cuts a lemon, slices and dices food, spins a lettuce, and squeezes the lemon on to the fish. He then goes to the bathroom, folds the toilet paper into a point, and puts the seat down.

Scene 18 Interior – Kim and Brett's unit – Day

We hear a crash from the kitchen.

Kath
>That's a stupid place to put the pots, Kim. And Brett, could you please come and open this cask of chardonnay ...

Kim
>You tell her. She loves you.

Brett
>No way. You tell her.

Kim
>She's really getting up my goat, and that can't be good for the baby. Mum, haven't you got a home to go to?

Kath
>What?

Kim
>Brett and me need some space.

Kath
>Oh, well I was just about to do some mince for Cujo, but I'll go, Kim, gosh. I've got a million things to do, actually, yes. No, I'll go. Gotta decant the dipping sauce, and ... yes. Goodbye, Brett.

Brett
> Yeah, I'll see you, Kath. Yeah.

Kath
> Bye, Kim.

Kim
> Actually, the yellow and the white and the pink poofs go really nice together.

Brett
> Yeah.

Brett moves to kiss Kim.

Kim
> Don't.

Scene 19 Interior – Kath's house – Day

Kath arrives home to find Kel in the kitchen cooking up a storm.

Kath
> Kel!

Kel
> Surprise! I've done the Iain Hewitson. You don't have to lift a finger.

Kath
> Iain Hewitson?

Kath
> But I was doing the Donna Hay tonight! I had it all organised. Oh, just forget it.

Kel
> Kath?

Scene 20   Interior/Exterior – Kath's house/front – Day

Kel
Kath? What's the matter? Come on. Open the door. You're being silly.

Kath
I'm not being silly, Kel. Don't say that.

Kel
Kath, what have I done? I'm wracking my brains here. I've cooked your tea, I've pressed your smalls, I've cleaned.

Kel
Is there something I haven't done?

Kath
It's not what you haven't done, Kel, it's what you have done. Everything. I mean, what am I left to do? Chop liver?

Kel
I'm sorry, Kath. I ... I was just trying extra hard 'cause I ... I didn't want you to think that you'd married a slob. I'm sorry.

Kath opens the door and gets out.

Kath
Oh Kel, I'm sorry too. It's just, I mean, I like to be kept busy, Kel, and now you're around, you do everything. I mean, you're just so capable. *(Neighbour walks past)* Oh yes, hello. We're fine, thank you.

Kel
Come on. Let's go inside. My cod's getting cold. You know, you're not completely useless yourself, Mrs. Kath Day-Knight.

Kath
I know. I'm terribly useful. I was just fishing.

Kel
Useful, eh? And what would you be useful at?

Kath
    Lots of things. Never you mind.

Kel
    Ohh! Come here, foxy.

Kath
    Oh, you great hunk-o'-spunk.

Kim comes up the path.

Kim
    Come on!

Kath
    Kim! What are you doing here? What's happened?

Kim
    Oh, what am I doing here? I'll tell you what I'm doing here. Brett cut down the tree outside the kitchen, it fell on the roof and now there's a huge hole.

Kath
    Oh no! What about poor Brett? Is he alright?

Kim
    I don't know. He hurt his neck or something. What about me? I can't stay there!

Kath
    Oh Brett, look at you! Put those bags down. Come on, come inside.

Brett
    Thanks, Mrs. D.

Kath
    Oh, we'll get a towel for you, quick! Kimmy! Come on. Oh, come and have a nice cup of Jarrah, Brett.

Kim
    Oh, he's putting that on. It was not like that at home.

Kath
Kim, can you please go and get a wheat bag and put it in the microwave? Kel, put those down, upstairs, and get a boomerang pillow from my bedroom please. Toot sweet. Come on.

Scene 21   Interior – Kath's house – Night

Brett
Yeah, it was crazy, Kath. It was like eighty or ninety knot breeze. It was like a willy willy.

Kath
You don't have to eat it, Kim. It's not very nice.

Kel
Take that?

Kath
Oh, that was beautiful. Thank you, Kel.

Kath
Have one of my cold rolls, Kimmy.

Kim
Yeah, I'll have one in a minute.

Kath
They're really nice. Sorry, Brett. Go on with your story.

Brett
Yeah, so the tree came down, and a root snapped off and punctured the water mains. Flooded the whole unit. It has to be gutted.

Kath
Oh, well that's nice, isn't it?

Kim
Mum!

Kath
Well it means you can do everything properly, you know, from the ground up. Put in your abducted heating and so forth.

Kim
Oh, abducted heating.

Kath
Yeah, abducted's nice.

Kim
It is nice.

Kath
It is. It's nice.

Kim
It is. It's different.

Kath
It is.

Kim
It's unusual.

Sharon enters covered in blood.

Sharon
Hi, everyone.

Kath
Sharon!

Kel
You're back early.

Sharon
Yeah, I was shot and captured in the first five minutes. So I was tied up for the rest of the time.

Kim
Did you get my present?

Sharon
Kim, I was being captured and tortured. I couldn't get to the shops.

Kim
> Oh, don't worry about me. Selfish.

Kath
> Oh, Sharon.

Sharon
> Actually, it wasn't as much fun as I thought it would be, Mrs. D, so I came home early.

Kel
> How about I run a nice spa for you, Sharon? *(To Brett and Kim)* And I'll make up the fold out for you two in the good room.

Brett
> Oh thanks, Kel.

Kath
> Excuse me. I think I would like to make up the fold out, if you don't mind.

Kel
> Sorry, Kath. Your call.

Kath
> Yes. Got to watch you.

Sharon
> Kim, are you ... are you going to eat that?

Kim
> Yes.

Kel
> Sharon, would you like some of my cod?

Sharon
> Oh, yeah. Yeah.

Kel
> Stay right there.

Sharon
> You get surprisingly hungry, actually, when you're tied up.

Kath *(whispers)*
No! No, Sharon, don't. It's not very nice.

Scene 22 Interior – Kath's house – Day

Kath
I've got two ham and two pressed chicken.

Kath *(voiceover)*
Kel and I have ironed out our little niggles. Communication is the key, I feel. And I have to say, we're right in sync with each other now. It's all about tolerance.

Kath
Yeah, go and get ready.

Kath has a Richmond beanie and scarf.

Kath
Come on, Kel! We don't want to miss our first footy match together, doll.

Kath *(voiceover)*
No. Each to their own, that's what I say.

Kel comes in wearing a Swans beanie and scarf.

Kath
Oh! Get out. Get out of my house!

Scene 23 Exterior – Kath's house/backyard – Day

Kath
We thrashed them, and now he's inside, sulking. I mean, I knew we would. I told him that. After I got over my initial shock and horror.

Kim
I reckon you should get a pool out here, Mum. You know, you've got the space.

Kath
>No. I don't like getting my hair wet, Kim. Goes all frizzy.

Kim
>Oh, this olive's stuffed.

Kath
>Throw it away. Now tell me, Kim. I am fascinated to know what happened with the tile guy you got, because he was so cheap I couldn't believe it.

Kim
>Oh well, you get what you pay for.

Kath
>Mm.

Kim
>He was always asking for coffees. I mean, how many coffees are you meant to give them? One in the morning, or one at every break? I mean, it's really hard.

Kath
>Oh Kim, read between the lines. It's just the human contact he craves. I mean, the poor guy's probably lonely stuck up there on the roof all day.

Kim
>I tell you what, though. I am loving myself sick in my new look unit. I've got such good taste.

Kath
>Oh, tickets. Speaking of that, do you want to come and see 'Hair' with me?

Kim
>Oh, hold on.

Kath
>Because I love David Atkins.

The Moon

❀ Kim and Sharon go to their school reunion
❀ Sharon has a new best friend
❀ Kath and Kel go on their honeymoon to Tulla

Scene 1 Interior – Computacity – Day

Brett is on the phone to Kim, and frantically trying to serve customers. He is talking to Kim but it looks as though he is talking to a customer.

Brett
(Into phone) I love you. I do. Oh, don't be like that. *(To customer)* Mate, your receipt. *(To new customer)* Welcome to Computacity super sellout sale. Well, stay at your Mum's. You know I have to work the next forty eight hours straight. I'm flat out. It's crazy stupid here, Kim.

Scene 2 Interior – Brett and Kim's unit – Day

Kim is on the phone and lying down on the settee.

Kim
I'm flat chat here myself, Brett. I'm pregnant, you know. I can't do much anymore. Alright, bye. Sharon!

Sharon
Yes? What?

Kim
Can you pass me the Tiny Teddies?

Sharon stares at the Tiny Teddies, just in front of Kim.

Sharon
> They are right there, Kim.

Kim
> I'm not s'posed to do any heavy lifting.

Sharon
> Oh, is that what the doctor said?

Kim
> No, the nail tech.

Sharon
> Oh. Oh, come on, Kim! I don't want to go to the school reunion on my own! It will be fun!

Kim
> Oh yeah, like last time, when I was completely humiliated turning up in fancy dress.

Sharon
> Oh Kim, that was just a few of the girls having a little bit of a joke. They were laughing at you, not with you. Oh come on.

Kim
> I said I'd think about it! I'll have to check if it's okay for the baby to hang around a bunch of loser girls.

Sharon
> Well what about me? I'm not a loser.

Kim
> Red hair, no friends.

Sharon
> Nicole Kidman's got friends.

Kim
> Has she, Sharon? Hey, that was my last Cheezy Stringer!

Sharon
> Well I didn't know!

Kim
> Oh well, you never bloody know! Now pass me my drink and then you can go and get my dry cleaning.

Sharon
Oh no, I can't, Kim. I've got a shift at the repat.

Kim
Oh right, I'll go. Ow!

Kim goes to get up.

Sharon
Oh my God, Kim, no, don't. Look I ... I'll see if I can get someone else to take my shift, alright? I'll do it. I'll go.

Kim
Good. You can drop me at Mum's on the way.

Kim
Sharon!

Sharon
Yes?

Kim
My bag!

Sharon
Oh, sorry Kim.

Scene 3   Interior – Kath's house *(Kitchen)* – Day

Kath is reading travel brochures and is on the phone.

Kath *(on phone)*
The garden room? Mm? And will you throw in a fruit platter with that, Chris? Alright. Email me the details. Bye.

Kim
Who's Chris when he's at home?

Kath
He's my travel agent, Kim. I'm trying to book Kel's and my honeymoon we never had. You know, the Daintree Eco tour.

Kath
    What are you doing? Don't touch that please, Kim.

Kim
    I'm looking for my school annual.

Kath
    Hey, get off the credenza! Look, why don't you go home to Brett, for God's sake?

Kim
    Because Brett's not there. He's working. I'm bored.

Kath
    Well you've got Sharon. Hang out with Sharon.

Kim
    Oh, whoop de do. Sharon. Wow.

Kath
    The way you treat, Sharon, really! You're skating on thin ice. And I think with the weight you're carrying, you're likely to fall right through.

Kim
    Here it is. Fountain Lakes State School. Ow, bugger!

Kath
    Kim! Keep your voice down. Kel's in the good room trying to do his quarterly BAS state, you know.

Kim
    His what?

Kath
    The GST. He's working out how much disposable income, if any, we've got for our honeymoon.

Kim dials the telephone.

Kim
    (Into phone) Hi, Sharon? Where are you? Yeah, I forgot something. Listen, you need to get me some hair twisties. Don't go to the salon on the mezzanine. Go downstairs to Hair-larious and haggle. Alright. And hurry up.

Kath
> Oh, leave poor Sharon alone, Kim. You know, people don't like being told what to do all the time.

Scene 4   Interior – Kath's house *(Good room)* – Day

Kath moves into the good room, where Kel is working on his BAS. Kath looks over his shoulder.

Kath
> No, Kel, you haven't added March!

Kel
> Oh, bum.

Kath
> And you have to separate all the crumbs off the schnitzels, because they attract their own ten percent.

Kel
> Kath, I know what I'm doing.

Kath
> And you put your dill in the wrong column. All herbs are the same. Miscellaneous foodstuffs.

Kel
> Kath, can you leave it, please?

Kath
> And sausage meat being a composite, that has to be cleared by all the individual manufacturers.

Kel
> Kath!

Kath
> I'm sorry, doll. Look, I ... I just need to know, you know, for the Daintree Eco Lodge, what our budget is. Are we going garden room, or can we afford the beachfront?

Kel
> We won't be going anywhere unless I get this BAS done. Now buzz off!

Kath
Alright. Won't say another word.

Kel
Bloody Howard!

Kath
You voted for him.

Scene 5   Interior – Fountain Gate Mall – Day

Sharon is at Fountain Gate, walking through the mall. She is carrying Kim's dry-cleaning. She is speaking on her mobile phone.

Sharon
Yeah, I've got it, Kim. I'm on my way back now. Okay, bye bye. Bye.

The phone rings again. Sharon answers thinking it is Kim again.

Sharon
Kim, I said I'm on my wa –... hello? Yes, this is the Sharon Strezlecki who was form four netball captain. Oh! Lisa-Marie Birkinshtocked! Oh! How are you?

Scene 6   Interior – Kath's house *(Kitchen/livingroom)* – Day

---

Kim is looking at her school annual. She looks at the various adolescent faces of her school friends.

Kim
Single. Single. Single. Loser. Ackers. Desperado.

Meanwhile, Kath is on the phone and looking at the computer.

Kath
No, no, no, Chris. Not the Japanee breakfast. I just have continental, and Kel just has yoghurt and muesli. Is that any cheaper? Great. Okay, book 'em Danno. Okay Chris. Yeah, see ya later. Bye. Good. It's done.

Sharon enters with all the dry-cleaning.

Kim
> Oh, where have you been?

Sharon
> Hi, Kim. I've got your stuff.

Kim looks through the dry-cleaning and is angry.

Kim
> They're not my good pants. They're knickerbockers, Sharon, you stupid bloody oaf!

Sharon
> I am not stupid, Kim. I couldn't see.

Kim
> Well where are my good pants? Oh God. These are Collette Dinnigans.

Sharon
> Sorry, Kim. I'll take them back.

Kim
> No, it's alright. I'll, ah, take 'em back. Later. Maybe.

Kath
> How is your eye, Sharon?

Sharon
> Well, it's not weeping anymore.

Kath
> Oh, give us a look. Oh look, that's looking much better. I reckon you could do without the patch now.

Sharon
> Oh, okay.

Kath
> Yeah, you don't want to become reliant.

Sharon
> Oh, hey, anyway, guess what, Kim? Remember Lisa-Marie Birkinshtocked from primary school?

Kim
> The fat kid who couldn't speak English?

Sharon
> She had just arrived here from Germany, Kim.

Kath
> I remember her. Poor little bugger. And you were the only one who was nice to her, Sharon.

Sharon
> Yeah. Well, anyway, she's coming down from the Gold Coast.

Kath
> Yeah, Lisa-Marie. Lovely girl. Big face. Looked just like Agnetha out of ABBA.

Sharon
> Yeah.

Kim
> No, no, no, no, no. I looked like Agnetha out of ABBA. She looked like Frida.

Sharon
> Well anyway, guess what, Kim? Me and Lisa-Marie are going to the school reunion together.

Kim imitates Sharon.

Kim
> 'Me and Lisa-Marie are going to the school reunion together.'

Kath rolls her eyes and looks away.

Kim
> What?

Kath
> Nothing. I just think it's very nice that Sharon's linked up with an old friend.

Kim
> Oh, hello! She already has an old friend. Who am I, chopped liver? Anyway, come on, Sharon. Let's get those, ah, hair twisties. I want to go upstairs and you can curl my hair Beyonce Knowles style.

Kath
Beyonce Knowles? Beyonce Knowles on cortisone!

Sharon
Ah, I can't actually, Kim. I've gotta pick up Lisa from the airport. And then ah, I'm gonna take her for lunch at the Docklands, and after that, we're going to Federation Square, to go to the Harry Potter gallery. Oh, it's gonna be ace. I can't wait. I gotta go.

Kim
Sharon!

Kath
Alright, that's done. Okay, I'm going to Fountain Gate to look for my new tropical story.

Kim
W-well, what am I s'posed to do?

Kath
Oh, I don't know, Kim. Oh, alright. You can come with me. Here you go. You can be my third eye. Come on, toot sweet. Out you go. Bye, Kel. Ta ta.

Kel
Bum!

Scene 7   Interior – Fountain Gate Mall – Day

Kath and Kim are shopping.

Kath
Oh Kim, it's going to be fantastic. Like the first day, we've got the crocodile farm, and then there's the Daintree River cruise, which includes coffee slash tea and biscuits, then there's the eco walks.

Kim notices an item of clothing on display.

Kim
Oh Mum, Mum, look at this. That peasant blouse. That's nice.

Kath
　Oh, is that peasant or pirate, Kim?

Kim
　Oh, pirate! You're so five minutes ago. It's peasant.

Kath
　Oh peasant, that's you, isn't it?

Kim
　Yeah.

Kath
　Yes, and there's nothing more flattering, I feel, than a puffy sleeve on a big lass.

Kim
　Yeah, I might get it.

Kath
　Yeah, good idea. Cover your fudubadahs, and your tum.

Kim
　Oh, anything else I need to cover up?

Kath
　Well, there's your welcome mat, your love handles and your dowager's hump, Kim.

Kim
　Mum!

Kath
　'Umour! I'm using 'umour. Now go and get it. Come on. It's a nice price, too.

Scene 8　Interior – Kath's house *(Good room/livingroom)* – Day

Kel is still doing his BAS, punching numbers in the calculator and getting frustrated. Kel is nearing the end of a long adding-up.

Kath
　And these were twenty five percent off, so that's only sixty three ninety-nine, and then the blouse was only forty which is good, wasn't it? That's cheap!

Kel
> Kath! Oh bum, I've lost my place.

We follow Kath as she moves from the good room through to the livingroom. Kim is going through the old school yearbook again, categorising each person.

Kim
> Sales – sales – marketing – sales.

Kath
> Oh, you should go to the reunion, Kim.

Kim
> Oh, look at Lisa-Marie Birkinshtocked. Talk about whacked with the ugly stick.

Kath
> Oh. Remember how Sharon and Lisa were thick as thieves at one stage?

Kim
> No, Mum, I was thick as a thieve! *(Speed dials)* Sharon, it's me again. If you get this message, can you disregard the others and call me back asap, if not before? It's Kim.

Kath
> Yeah, they were such good mates. Joined at the hip.

Kim
> No, they weren't!

Kath
> I'm going to just try these on.

Kath leaves.

Kim
> Mole. Mole. Virgin. Mole.

The Moon

Scene 9   Interior – Kath's house *(Good room)* – Day

Kath
> Mm, I like these Kumffs. And this hemp tracksuit'll be good. It breathes.

Kel
> Bad news, sweets. The honeymoon's off, I'm afraid.

Kath
> What, Kel? But I just had the new fantasy spray on tan! It was fifty five dollars, plus GST. What's happened?

Kel
> You said it, Kath. Three little words. GST. It's killing me. I don't know. It just seems I haven't got two brazoos to rub together.

Kath
> Well I have. I mean, we've got my *(She pulls up her face to look like a facelift)*... money.

Kel
> No, we're not dipping into that. You ... you might need it.

Kath
> Well not for a few years, I hope.

Kel
> No, no, I'm sorry love. I just reckon we can't do it. Not ... not this year. Oh, makes me so flamin' mad. I mean, I'd like to see John Howard do pork and dill for less than five ninety nine a kilo.

Kath
> Oh, don't worry, Kel. Doesn't matter. We'll just stay home. I mean, what's the big deal? Let it go, Kath. Let it go.

Kim comes in, reading a letter, then notices Kath is distressed.

Kim
> Mail's here. It's for me. What's the matter, Mum?

The Moon

Kath
> We've just had to cancel the once in a lifetime Eco Tour honeymoon, Kim.

Kim
> Hey, look at this!

Kath
> Not now, Kim. Your timing's way out.

Kim
> No, no, Mum. Remember when I had to run up your credit card bill to get you enough fly buys to get you a free mystery flight? It's come through.

Kath
> Oh, give me a look! Where are we going? Oh, Kel! Kel, the mystery flight! Oh! Where are we going? Yes, Kyabram, Kel!

Kel
> Kath!

Kath
> Kim, Kyabram!

Kel
> Kyabram!

Kel
> Thanks, Kim.

Kath
> Oh, when do we fly? Oh, tomorrow night, Kel!

Kel
> We can do it, love. Action stations

Kath
> Okay, I need to get my wheel on. My vanity, my backpack, my day pack and my bum bag. Okay, if anyone needs me, I'm in the root.

Kel
> Look out all you Kyabram carp! Kel Knight's a-coming!

The Moon

Kath
> Oh, it's so exciting, Kel. I love Kyabram.

Kath and Kel exit in a flurry of excitement. Kim is left alone.

Kim
> But I ... I can't spend Saturday night on my own. What would that look like? Mum?

Kim
> *(Into phone)* Sharon? If you can drag yourself away from Lisa-Marie for five minutes and get this message, you'll know that yes, I am going to come to the reunion tomorrow night, and this time, I'm going to wipe the floor with what I'm wearing. It's Kim.

Scene 10 Interior – Kath's house *(Bedroom/upstairs hall)* – Day

---

Kath is calling to Kel in the roof.

Kath
> Oh Kel, can you get my rod out too, please?

Kel
> No worries.

Kim
> Mum?

Kim enters Kath's bedroom in her peasant blouse, with pink twisty curlers in her hair.

Kim
> Ta da! I look like one classy peasant.

Kath
> Well, yeah. That looks nice, love.

Kim
> I think I look like Rachel Hunter.

Kath
> Well, you look like some sort of Hunter. Where'd you get those pants?

Kim
> They're Collette Dinnigan's knickerbockers.

Kath
> Mm, they're cool.

Kim walks out of the bedroom. Kel is carrying his fishing rod he pokes Kim in the eye.

Kim
> Ow! Oh my God, Kel, you fool!

Kath
> Kimmy, are you alright? Oh Kimmy, oh Kimmy, it's just a graze. It's just a graze.

Kim
> Oh, what about the reunion!

Kath
> Oh Kimmy, Kimmy, look at me, please. Look at me. Look at me.

Kel
> I can't!

Kath
> Use your other eye. Now I've got one word to say to you, Kim. Sharon's flesh coloured eye patch.

Scene 11 Exterior – Reunion function venue – Day

Sharon
> Kim, oh my God! It's not fancy dress.

Kim
> What do you mean? I'm not in fancy dress. Bloody heels!

Sharon
> You look like a pirate!

Kim
> I do not! As if! As if anyone else is gonna think that.

Lisa has not heard this exchange.

Lisa
　Ahoy, Kim!

Sharon
　Oh Kim, you remember Lisa?

Lisa
　Love the eye patch, Pirate Pete.

Kim
　Excuse me. I'm not a pirate. I have hurt my eye.

Lisa
　I've got the exact same knickerbockers. Size six?

Kim
　Yeah, six ... *(Sotto voce)* teen.

Lisa
　And what about Sharon? How good does she look? Sharon, I'm going to get you a drink. What do you want?

Sharon
　Oh, appletini, thanks Lisa.

Woman
　Ahoy there, Horatio Hornblower.

Kim
　Excuse me! Horatio Hornbag!

Scene 12 Interior – Airport – Day

Kath and Kel are at the check-in counter.

Man *(on two way)*
　No, they've only just gone into a meeting with management.

Staff member
　Alright, Guy. Yes? *(To Kath and Kel)* Sorry about this.

Man *(on two way)*
　Phil? Phil, can you hear me?

Staff member
> Hello? No, look, I'm terribly sorry, sir. It seems all the air traffic controllers have walked off the job. All domestic flights are grounded until further notice. I am sorry.

Kel
> Why? What's the problem?

Staff member
> Well I can't tell you exactly, but it seems to be GST related.

Kel
> Bloody Howard!

Kath
> Oh, I won't say it.

Staff member
> Look, Guy, can you hear me?

Man *(on two way)*
> Phil, can you hear me?

Kel
> Will there be any chance of an upgrade?

Staff member
> No. Guy, I can't hear you. Are you there?

Kel
> I guess we'll just have to wait.

Kath
> Oh, it's a bugger, doll.

Kel
> Go for a bit of walk.

Kath
> Oh, there's the Australis Shop over there. I might go and look for a new sponge bag.

The Moon

Scene 13 Interior – Airport – Night

Kath and Kel enjoying the airport. They are looking at DVDs and magazines.

Kel
Here, pass those up.

Kath
Have a Wet One, doll, for after.

Kel
Yep, no worries.

Kath
Oh, where's my camera? Oh, there it is.
Take a photo of us.

Kel
Oh, terrific.

Kath
I've grabbed this very good book. I'm going to read that.

Kel and Kath go into the souvenir store.

Kath
Did you see those mouse pads? The mouse pads are great. You need a new mouse pad.

Kel
Oh, righto.

Kath
Oh, look at this. What a huge range of Coogis they've got.

We see Kath and Kel walking along in matching Coogi jumpers.

Kel
Kath, come on. Up here. This is great. You hungry?

Kath
Oh, a little bit.

Kel
We'll grab something to eat.

Scene 14 Interior – Reunion function venue – Night

Kim
I was not Frida.

Sharon
One thing's for sure. I was not Frida.

Kim
No, you were Benny and Bjorn 'cause you look like them. I was Agnetha!

Lisa
You were Frida.

Kim
I'm going home. Come on, Sharon.

Sharon
No, no, Kim. Um, I don't want to.

Kim
Excuse me?

Lisa
Where do you want to go, Sharon? Do you want to go home, or do you want to stay?

Kim
Excuse me, Lisa. I think I'll be the one to tell Sharon where to go.

Lisa
Sharon, have you told Kimmy the big news? Sharon is going to move up to the Gold Coast with me. She's going to try for the A.I.S.

Kim
What?

Sharon
That's right, Kimmy. Lisa is helping me to fulfil my lifelong dream of being an Olympic athlete. I'm flying up with her in a couple of days to check it out.

Lisa
    What do you think?

Kim
    What do I think? I'll tell you what I think. I think you can stick the A.I.S. right up your A.I.S.E.!

Sharon
    Kimmy! Kim, wait!

Scene 15   Interior – Airport/Qantas Club – Night

Kath
    Ohh, look at the buffet, Kel. And all for free.
    That's amazing.

Kel
    Free drinks as well. Juices, wine, whatever you want.

Kath
    Really?

Kel
    Yeah.

Kath
    Oh, gee. How the other half live.

Kel
    Come on, I've got this.

Kel and Kath walk into the club.

Kath
    Oh, I didn't know about that. Hello!

Attendant
    Excuse me, sir.

Kel notes the attendant's name badge: 'Liz'.

Kel
    Yes, ah, Liz. What can I do you for?

Attendant
    Can I just see your card?

Kel reluctantly hands over the card to the attendant.

Attendant
I am sorry, sir. We don't accept Video Ezy cards.

Kel
Okay. Thanks.

Kath
Oh, Kel!

The attendant talks to some new customers, and Kath and Kel sneak in.

Scene 16 Exterior – Reunion function venue – Night

Sharon catches up with Kim, who is leaving the function on her own.

Sharon
Kim, wait! Kim, are you crying?

Kim
No! Your eye patch is rubbing my eye.

Sharon
Oh, sorry

Kim
Some second best friend you turned out to be. I can't believe you're leaving me in my condition. The one time I ask you to do something for me ...

Sharon
Kim, this is my big chance. Lisa feels like she owes me. She says I've been like a rock for her.

Kim
But you're my rock.

Sharon
Yeah, well, now I'm Lisa's rock as well.

Kim
Well how many people's rocks are you?

Sharon
Well, I'm your rock. I'm Lisa's rock, I'm your Mum's rock sometimes. Kel says I'm a good stick, which is kind of like a rock.

Kim
Well I don't reckon that makes you a rock, Sharon. I reckon that makes you gravel.

Sharon
Take that back. I am not gravel!

Kim
Gravel, gravel!

Sharon
Frida, Frida!

Lisa
Sharon!

Sharon
Goodbye, Kim.

Sharon goes back inside to join Lisa and the others. Kim is left alone.

Scene 17 Interior – Airport/Qantas Club – Day

Kath and Kel enjoying The Qantas Club lounge. Kel piling his plate with food and returning again and again. Kath selecting magazines. Fine dining with tiny plates, low tables and plastic knives.

Kath
Australia Telecom ... Telecommunications and Convergence News magazine. Yeah, might be nice.

Kath
These dolmades are very nice.

Kel
Mm.
What's this stuff here?

Scene 18 Interior – Kath's house – Day

> **Kim** *(voiceover)*
> Yep, I now realise I didn't treat Sharon the way I should have.

Kim is depressed and lonely, looking at a photo of her and Sharon in happier days. In the photo Sharon is cowering.

> **Kim** *(voiceover)*
> I mean, calling her a great bloody oaf all the time. Maybe she didn't like that. I didn't know. She didn't say anything.

Scene 19 Exterior – Airport – Day

Kath and Kel leave the airport.

> **Kath**
> Oh, there's a Skybus.

> **Kel**
> Yep, there it is.

> **Kath**
> I hope it waits for us.

> **Kel**
> We'll be right.

> **Kath**
> Hello. Wait for us.

As Kath and Kel leave the airport, Lisa and Sharon arrive by taxi

> **Sharon**
> Oh wow, Lisa, this is so exciting.

> **Kel**
> I think this'll drop us off in the right spot. Yeah, yeah ...

> **Kath**
> I'm Kath.

Damien
    I'm Damien.

Kath
    Oh, hi Jamie.

Kel
    Pleased to meet you.

Kath
    Yeah, we've been shopping. We've had a ball.

Damien
    I can see that.

Kel
    Hey, you can't leave that there.

Sharon
    You sure you don't want me to get that?

Lisa
    No, Sharon, you're not touching a thing.

Scene 20   Interior – Kath's house – Day

Kel shows Brett their photos.

Kel
    That's Kath on the escalators.

Brett
    Great shot.

Kel
    And that's where we had breaky every morning.

Brett
    Hey, nice. Yeah.

Kim
    Sharon still hasn't called.

Brett
    Oh, don't worry, Kim. You still got me.

Kath
> Oh, was this the new Enya CD we bought on our honeymoon?

Kel
> Yep.

Kath
> Oh, takes me back.

Kath and Kel *(singing)*
> Sail away, sail away, sail away.

Kel
> You know what? I reckon it was the perfect honeymoon. I'll remember it as long as I live.

Kath
> Oh ditto, doll. And you know, Kim? What a nong I was to think you had to get on a plane and go somewhere.

Kim
> What, so you just dagged around the airport for two days?

Kel
> Got it in one, Kim.

Kath
> Oh, it wasn't daggy, Kim. It was cool. I mean, it's all there at Tullamarine. The Australis Counter, Chocolate Box.

Kel
> The internet café.

Kath
> Oh, I went insane in Sanity. And you know, any time you wanted a bit of P and Q, you know, to get away from it all, you just took the moving walkway half a kilometre up the concourse to gate lounge twenty six.

Kel
> I even got a tan through the plate glass watching the planes being grounded.

Kath
>Yeah, it's a nice colour, too. It's natural.

Kel
>Yeah. Now we've just gotta pay for it. Better get back to my BAS.

Kath
>Yes. I'll bring your Jarrah in to you, doll.

Kel
>No worries.

Kim
>I guess I've learnt my lesson. As they say in the ABBA song, I've met my Waterloo. Sometimes I think I'm my own worst enemy.

Brett
>Don't be silly, Kim. You've got heaps worser enemies. I'm gonna miss Sharon too. She was a good egg.

Kim
>She was my rock.

Kath
>Yeah. She was a pillar of salt to all of us.

Kim goes to the microwave and gets out a huge plate of footy franks. Kath glares at her.

Kath
>Oh! No, Kim, no!

Kim
>What?
>I'm depressed.

Kath
>Oh look, eating footy franks is not going to bring Sharon back.

The screen door opens and Sharon comes in.

Sharon
>Something smells great. Hi, everyone.

Brett
    Hi, Sharon.

Kath
    Sharon.

Sharon
    Hi, Kim.

Kim
    Hi, Sharon.

Kath, being discreet, motions to Brett.

Kath
    Brett? I need you in the roof, toot sweet.

Brett leaves with Kath.

Kim
    Would you like a footy frank?

Sharon can't believe her ears.

Sharon
    Me? Really?

Kim
    Yeah, go on.

Sharon
    Oh, thanks, Kim.

Kim
    What are you doing here?

Sharon
    I've left Lisa.

Kim
    What happened?

Sharon
    Well, we were waiting for the plane at the gate lounge, but ... I just couldn't handle it.

Kim
    Why?

Sharon
Quite frankly, I didn't care for the way she spoke to me.

Kim
Like what? What'd she say?

Sharon
Oh, you know. She was always on and on at me all the time about how talented I am, and how my friends don't appreciate me.

Kim
That does sound weird.

Sharon
Yeah. So I high tailed it out of there and came straight back here.

An awkward pause.

Sharon
I missed you, Kim.

Sharon goes to take another footy frank.

Kim
I said 'one'! Put that back. I said one. They're for me. I've got morning sickness. I need to eat –

Sharon
Well, I didn't know!

Kim
You never bloody know, Sharon!

Sharon
I thought there was another packet –

Kim
Well you're not here for five minutes and you're eating us out of house and home –

Sharon
Oh, right. You know I have to eat every three hours –

Kim
I don't know everything – about you.

Sharon
– Kim. You know that they don't serve meals on Skybus.

Kim
The way you treat us!

Sharon
Oh, you act like I do!

Kath rushes in as Sharon and Kim start to fight.

Kath
Time out, time out, time out, please! Now Kimmy, Kimmy. Look at me, please. Look at me. Now Sharon, look at me. Now Kim, look at Sharon. And Sharon, look at Kim. Now both look at me, please. Now I got one word to say to you. Reconciliation.

Kel
Bloody Howard!

Scene 21 Exterior – Kath's house/backyard – Day

Kath is reading a magazine.

Kim
What are you reading?

Kath
Mystic Meg. Do you want to know your stars?

Kim
Ooh, ooh, yes. Yes, yes, yes, yes.

Kath
Alright, Scorpio. *(Reads)* 'A hectic work and social calendar means you sometimes forget to eat. Keep some low fat snacks in your desk drawer to pick at during the day.' If you had a desk drawer, Kim. 'Your naturally bubbly personality and your caring nature sees you sometimes giving too much.
This week, think about yourself for a change.'

Kim
>Oh, she's good. She's ... that's me. Here. Do you wanna know yours?

Kath
>Alright, Leo.

Kim
>What are you? Leo, Leo, Leo. Okay. *(Reads)* 'Being Leo the lion, your pride is in your beautiful mange of hair.'

Kath
>Mm.

Kim
>That's right.

Kath
>That's right.

Kim
>'But this week will see your usually lustrous locks take a battering. You might like to try a new style. Something short and neat, for example, might win back that certain someone's wandering eye.' Whoo!

Kath
>Oh, what a load of bunkum. What planet are you on, Mystic Meg? All bound for coo coo land.

Kim
>I think she's good.

Kath
>Speaking of which, I know I keep banging on about the trip, Kim, but I really have the bug, I tell you.

Kim
>Oh, yuk!

Kath
> The travel bug. No, I feel while Kel and I still can, I want to see the world. So next, we're going to go to Mascot, Esserdon. That's a day trip. After that, who knows, Kim? Nagoya. Gatwick is meant to be beautiful.

Kim
> Ow!

Obsession

4

- Kel and Kath are on a no-carb diet
- Sharon tries to Irish dance back into Mark's heart
- Brett vies for promotion
- Kim becomes a corporate trophy wife

Scene 1 Interior – Kath's house *(Bedroom)* – Night

Kel is moving about in bed, groaning. Kath gets into bed next to him.

Kel
Oh, bed! So good!

Kath
Oh I know, Kel. I am so tired after all that boxercising. So sore!

Kel
So tired!

Kath
Oh, ditto doll, big time.

Kel
Sweets, I don't know about this get fit campaign. I mean, why bother when it means I haven't got the energy to satisfy my lovely lady?

Kath
Oh well Kel, I'm not exactly Carmen Sutra myself tonight. Alright, nigh-nigh, doll.

Obsession

Scene 2   Interior – Kath's house *(Kitchen)* – Day

Kath is popping a myriad of pills.

> **Kath** *(voiceover)*
> Evening primrose, my Promensil, B12, Omega three.

She picks up a health drink.

> **Kath** *(voiceover)*
> Yuk. Oh well, no pain, no gain.
>
> **Kath**
> Right, breaky. What day am I on? Day four, breakfast. Compote of yoghurt and nuts.
>
> **Kel**
> Morning, sweets.
>
> **Kath**
> Oh, speaking of nuts, hello you. Thank you for last night. I enjoyed that cuddle.
>
> **Kel**
> Oh, sorry love, it was all I could muster.
>
> **Kath**
> Oh, don't worry about it, doll. Now what can I get you for breaky? You're on day four. You can have an egg white, three prunes and a Yakult.
>
> **Kel**
> Thanks, sweets. I'd better get a wriggle on. I've got to go to gym.
>
> **Kath**
> Ooh! Who's Gym when he's at home?
>
> **Kel**
> Ooh, gettin' a little bit jealous, are you?
>
> **Kath**
> I might be.
>
> **Kel**
> Well there's no need.

They go to pash. Kim comes in.

Kim
> Oh, hello! Revolting.

Kel
> Hello, Kim.

Kath
> Gee, quarter to eight. Why bother going home at all, Kim? I may as well just set up the fold out for you in the good room, you're so keen on the place.

Kim
> Oh, as if I want to hang around a couple of old grogans. I just don't have any food in the fridge.

Kath
> Well, Kim, you'll get no joy in there. Kel and I are on the Doctor Cabot's no carbohydrate diet.

Kim is bent over at fridge, and makes a gobbling sound like a turkey.

Kath
> What's that s'posed to mean?

Kim
> It'll take more than not eating bread to get rid of your crepey neck and your turkey gobbler.

Kath
> Oh, you're a stupid girl.

Kim
> Pooh! What's this?

Kel
> Oh that's my acidopholos and bifidopholus.

Kath
> Yes, and you keep adophilous, please!

Kim
> Yeah, Brett forgot to leave me any food before he left. I'm about to go into ketosis.

Kath
> Oh! In your dreams.

Kim
> Can I've a spoon, please.

Kath
> Now can you tell me please, Kim, has Brett heard about his promotion yet?

Kim
> No. And he's such a wuss he won't ask. And they've had him working all weekend again.

Kath
> That's right. He's on his career projectory, Kim. Poor Brett.

Kim
> Poor Brett's been living La Vida Loca at the Grand Prix. I just don't see why he couldn't take me.

Kath
> He's entertaining in a corporate box, Kim. He's got to impress the clients.

Kim
> Well, who wouldn't be impressed by me?

Kath
> He needs a corporate wife, Kim. Someone who's good with people.

Kim with mouth full of yoghurt.

Kim
> Well I'm a people person. You know, I'm corporate. I could entertain those dickheads any day.

Kath
> You, Kim, are a liability for poor Brett. You know, if you just did a little bit more with your presentation, you could actually help Brett claw his way up that Computacity ladder.

Kim
> I know. I just couldn't be arsed.

Kim waves her bum.

Kim
> Could not be arsed.

Kel
> I'll be in the shower, Kath.

Kath
> Yes, alright, doll. Oh yes, very corporate. I mean, do you think that's the way Wendy Deng behaves to Mr. Murdoch's important clients in their New York penthouse? I don't think so. Kel?

Kim makes turkey gobbling sound.

Kath
> Kim, you're not impressing anybody.

Scene 3   Interior – Gym – Day

Kath and Kel are in a boxercise ring.

Kath *(voiceover)*
> Yes, holding back the years is a priority for me and Kel. What's so darned wrong with that? Kel is an Adonis. But unlike the Greek statue, things aren't exactly turning to stone at present. Which is ironical because somehow, I'm feeling totally shagged.

Scene 4   Interior – Kath's house *(Kitchen)* – Day

Kim is in kitchen reading a magazine and eating ice-cream.

Kim *(voiceover)*
> It's hard being a wife. There are so many choices. Corporate. House. Fish. Which one's me?

Sharon enters through sliding door.

Sharon
> Hi, Kim.

Kim
> Hi. Where have you been?

Sharon
> Oh, been at Mark's all night.

Kim
> Oh yeah, what'd you do?

Sharon
> Oh, you know. The usual. Waited outside in my car and then went through his rubbish. That looks nice. What's that?

Kim
> A billabong. Yummy.

Sharon
> Oh. Maybe I'll drown my sorrows in a Billabong.

Kim
> None left.

Sharon *(crying)*
> Nothing goes right.

Kim
> Oh well, boring. Places to meet. People to do.

Scene 5   Interior – Gym café – Day

Kath and Kel are having a smoothie at the gym café and reading magazines.

Kel
> I had a sexy ...

Woman walks to Kel and Kath with drinks.

Kel
> Thanks very much.

Kath
> Thank you.

Kel
> I had a sexy dream about you last night.

Kath
>Ooh, things are looking up, Kel. Do tell.

Kel
>Mmm. I dreamt you were a big loaf of Bornhoffen and I gobbled you all up.

Kath
>Oh, you are missing the carbs, aren't you? What do you think of the prostate smoothie?

Kel
>Oh, it's very nice.

Kath
>Mm, yes, I like it. And it's doing my prostate no end of good.

Kel
>Have a look at her. How does she look so young? She looks like a teenager.

Kath
>Oh, Kel, it's Nicky Webster. Of course she looks young. She's in show business. She's probably had work.

Kel
>Yeah, right.

Scene 6 Interior – Computacity – Day

Kim is sitting behind the counter as Brett is trying to serve customers.

Kim
>So, your boss. What'd he say?

Brett
>It's not a he, it's a she. Twenty nine, ninety-five thanks, mate. She says it's between me and Jared.

Kim
>Jared? You're kidding. You said he was a dick.

Brett
>Keep your voice down, Kim.

Kim
  Who's that?

Brett
  Shona, Jared's wife.

Kim
  What, his wife works here? That's weird.

Brett
  She manages software. She's really smart.

Kim
  She's bloody ugly. So what time's lunch?

Brett
  I'm working through lunch, Kim.

Kim notices Kelly, a young woman who obviously works at Computacity.

Kim
  Excuse me. What's your name?

Kelly
  Hi. Kelly.

Kim
  Well Kelly, could you get me a drink of water? I'm pregnant and I'm very thirsty.

Brett
  Kim, that's my boss.

Kelly
  Can I see you in my office, Brett?

Brett
  You'd better go, Kim. That's my interview

Kim is left alone. She abuses a customer.

Kim
  What are you staring at, stare bear?

Kim *(voiceover)*
> Look at Shona. She thinks she's God's gift, strutting around serving customers, just so Jared can get his promotion. But she doesn't know about Brett's secret weapon. Me.

Kim knocks sign over then walks out.

Kim *(voiceover)*
> I'm his biggest asset.

Scene 7 Exterior – Molly Bloom's pub – Night

Sharon is outside the pub looking in the window at Mark playing the fiddle and Moira, the river-dancer, dancing. 'What about me?' is playing.

Scene 8 Interior – Kath's house *(Kitchen)* – Day

Kath, wearing cream, is putting a mask on Kel.

Kath
> Yeah. It's an 'erbal face lift, Kel. Gets rid of all your bags, your jowls. You'll look ten years younger.

Kel
> What's in it?

Kath
> Oh, jojoba, hello Vera. Now, go and lie in the good room, read your Men's Health, take note of the sealed section. Very relevant.

Kim
> *(On phone)* Yeah.

Kim enters, talking on phone.

Kim
> What? Kelly said you're the favourite? Obviously I impressed her. Oh, you're so close, Brett, I can smell it. All you have to do is nobble Shona in software and I can help you whiteant Jared. Alright, get back to me. Bye.

Kath

Oh, what's all this, Kim?

Kim

I'm going to help Brett get his promotion. Mum, I'm going to be a corporate wife.

Kath

Oh, good girl. But you do realise you're going to have to schmooze bigwigs and work the room and such, Kim.

Kim

Easy-peasy lemon squeezy.

Kath

Oh, easy! I admire your chutzpah, Kim. I just hope you've got the why with all to back it up.

Kim

Mum, I've done the research. To be corporate, you've got to whiteant, back stab and be two faced. Hello?

Kath

Oh, point taken.

Kim

I've got to go shopping. If I'm going to do this properly, I'd better be a brand Nazi. If it's not Dotti or Witchery, don't talk to me.

Kath

Oh Kim, I've got a lot of power dressing shoulder pads up in the low boy.

Kim

Shoulder pads? Mum, you're so five minutes ago.

Kath

Oh.

Kim

No, I need to look at some magazines. Get some fashion ideas.

Kath
Oh, well I've got a lot of old *Ita*s in the toot. They're good.

Kim
No, Mum!

Kath
Ita's a great magazine.

Kim
I'll find something else.

Kath
If they still had it around. Very useful.

Sharon enters, depressed.

Kath
Oh, hi Sharon.

Sharon
Hi, Mrs. D.

Kath
You look tired, love. What's been happening?

Sharon
Oh, I just came off a double shift at the repat, and I happened to go past Molly Bloom's on the other side of town, and I saw Mark.

Kath
Oh, any hope?

Sharon
He was with the lovely leggy Moira.

Kath
Who?

Sharon
The lovely leggy Moira. She's a river dancer. He seems really smitten, Mrs. D. Oh, why doesn't he like me?

Kel comes in with his face mask on, and with the magazine.

Kel
> How long, sweets?

Kath
> Oh, you can take that all off now, Kel.

Kel
> All off, eh? Oh, that and the sealed section might just get me going, foxy.

Kath
> Oh.
> Yes, well we'll see.

Sharon
> You're so lucky, Mrs. D. Kel's all over you like a rash. What's your secret?

Kath
> Well Sharon, it's all in your peregnomes. I mean it's chemistry. I give off an aroma that does things to Kel. Sometimes.

Sharon
> Oh. Gee. Wonder what my aroma's doing to Mark?

Kim
> Nothing deodorant wouldn't cure.

Kath
> Oh, Kim! Buck up, Sharon.

Sharon
> What?

Kath
> I mean, get with the program. You know, read the signs. If Mark likes river dancing, you do river dancing. I mean, it's very popular these days.

Sharon
> Is it?

Kath
>Oh yes, and absolutely. And you should see the guys who do it. They are absolute pieces of Irish eye candy, the lot of them.

Kim
>I've heard those guys have to have sex the minute they come off stage.

Kath
>Oh, Kim!

Sharon
>Really?

Kath
>As if.

Kim
>Yeah.

Kath
>No, not after that sort of physical exertion. I mean, take it from someone who knows.

Kim
>Why don't you take up river dancing, Sharon? Get you out from under your own hairs.

Kath
>Yeah. Look, you're a good little mover. Give it a go.

Sharon
>Right. Maybe I will, Mrs. D.

Scene 9   Exterior – Kath's house/street – Day

Kel and Kath are power-walking down the court, almost at Kath's house.

Kath
>You know, Kel, it's bad enough that I'm going to be a grandmother, but I'm not going to be a wrinkly, pruney old one.

Kel
> That 'erbal facelift did nothing for me, Kath.

Kath
> No, you're right, Kel. You're still very jowly.

Kel
> I think I'm starvatious. I'd kill for just one slice of bread.

Kath
> Oh. Oh, look at the time, Kel. You've got to get to jazzercise. Your fluoro bike shorts are in the dryer.

Kel
> Okay.

Kath
> They should be dry by now. Oh, I'd better get a wriggle on, too. Sharon'll be here in a minute.

Scene 10 Interior – Kath's house *(Good room)* – Day

Kath is waiting for Sharon.

Kath
> Come on, Sharon. Have you got it on?

Sharon comes in, wearing an Irish river-dancing velvet dress. It is really short.

Sharon
> What do you think, Mrs. D?

Kath
> Mmm ...

Sharon
> Moira's looked different, somehow. It's a bit itchy, but I like it.

Kath
> Yeah. Ah, we could let it out a bit. I like the puffy sleeves. They cover your fudubudahs, which is good.

Sharon
> It's a bit split here.

Kath
Oh, well that's alright. You keep your arms down when you're doing Irish dancing.

Sharon
Oh, okay.

Kath
Yeah, go for a bit of a jig.

Sharon
Alright.

Sharon does some dancing. Her chest is bouncing.

Kath
Yeah. We might get you into a sports bra for this, I think, love.

Scene 11   Interior – Fountain Gate Mall/fashion shop – Day

Kim is in the change room, trying on her version of corporate outfit. She comes out to show assistant.

Kim *(voiceover)*
It's times like this, when you've got to think mentally. Brett needs me to get this promotion. You know, I've got the looks, but I've also got the smarts. Yep, like Rachel Hunter, I'm a foxy moron.

Kim
Oh, my husband Brett is going to go off when he sees me in this.

Assistant
Yes, I think he will.

Kim
Nuh.

Scene 12 Interior – Kath's house *(Good room)* – Day

Kath and Kel finish on their exercise machines. They get off. Kel is exhausted.

Kath
And, downhill. Telemark.

Kel
Ohh! Ohh! Can't keep doing this. It's ... killing me.

Kath
Oh, I know what you mean, Kel. I mean, we seem to be doing everything. I mean, the body's defying gravity. What about the face?

Kel
Oh, you're alright. Have a look at this. More chins than a Chinese phone book. I'm always knackered. There must be an easier way.

Kath
Well, I think there is, Kel. I mean, how does just going troppo on a couple of banana lounges sound?

Kel
Oh, keep talkin'. Keep talkin'.

Scene 13 Interior – Computacity – Day

It is Friday night drinks. Kim turns up. She looks around.

Kim *(voiceover)*
When Brett gets this new promotion, all this will be mine.

Kim
Hi, Brett.

Brett
Oh, Kim. What's up? What are you doing here?

Kim
I was just shopping. Thought I'd get a lift home.

Brett
Ah, we're having end of month drinks.

Kim
Oh, good. Hi, I'm Kimberley, and you are –

Jared
I'm Jared.

Kim
Ah, the famous Jared. I've heard all about you.

Jared
All good I hope?

Kim
No. I'll have a cardonnay, thanks Jared.

Brett
Don't drink wine, Kimmy. You know what you're like.

Kim
Shut up, Brett. The doctor said I could have one. Now I'm going to work the room. Watch and learn. Kelly! Empty glasses here! Not a good look.

Someone bumps in to Kim.

Woman
Sorry.

Kim
I could have you sacked for that. Oh look, Brett. Kelly's coming over. Look at her body English. She likes you. Let me do the talking. So, Kelly. Who does my husband have to root to get a promotion around here? Not you, I hope.

Scene 14   Interior – Kath's house *(Bedroom)* – Day

Kel and Kath are packing for the long weekend at the retreat.

Kath
Yeah, I've already packed your massage sandals, Kel. And your happy coat's still on the line.

Kel

Can you put these in your bag?

Kath

Oh, you won't need both, Kel. Just take that one. That's nice.

Kel

(Looking at pamphlet) This resort's pretty ritzy, by the looks. All the celebrities go there, do they?

Kath

Yeah, apparently. And not just B list. C list as well.

Kel

Ohh. Yeah, I can't help feeling we were a bit tragic back there. You know, a bit desperate with all our diets and exercise.

Kath

I know. I mean, who do we think we are? I mean, reality check, peoples. I mean, here's one out of the box. Why not age gracefully?

Scene 15 Interior – Computacity – Night

Later that night, Kim is working the room.

Kim

No, I think I'm right on that. I'm still waiting for my cardonnay.

Kelly

I think you mean chardonnay.

Kim

No, Kelly, it's French. The 'h' is silent.

Kelly

No, it's chardonnay, Kim.

Brett

It is chardonnay, Kim.

Jared
    Yeah, no, it's chardonnay.

Kim
    Oh, alright. Chardonnay, chardonnay, you pack of shunts!

Brett
    Kim!

Brett goes to shush Kim. She shrugs him off and falls into a bank of computers. We hear a crash.

Kim
    Ahh!

Scene 16   Interior – Health Resort – Day

By the pool, everyone is lying on banana lounges. They are all bandaged up, in bathrobes. Kath and Kel are meeting people.

Kel
    It's very nice, isn't it?

Kath
    Mm. It's quite ritzy.

Kel
    Anyway, cheers.

Kath
    Cheers, Kel.

Kath
    This mocktail's going down very nice.

Kel
    I tell you what, once these bandages come off, you'll be in real trouble. I'll be straight back on the horse, don't you worry.

Kath
    Who are you calling a horse? Though I have to say, I'm champing at the bit.

Kel
> *(Turns to another guest)* Hello. Where are you from?

Woman
> Oh, Sydney.

Kath
> Oh. Well, I'm from Melbourne, and Kel's an Adelaidian, originally.

Woman
> Oh, Rundle Mall.

Kel
> Yeah. Are you going into town for tea tonight?

Woman
> Oh, no. We're dining in.

Kath
> Yes. We're dining in tonight. Town can get a bit much, can't it?

Kel
> Would you like to join us for tea? We're having the pureed smorgasbord.

Woman
> Oh, yes.

Kath
> Alright. You could join us at our table, about seven. This is the life, isn't it? Ow!

Scene 17 Interior – Kath's house *(Bathroom)* – Day

Kim and Sharon are talking. Sharon is dressed in the Irish-dancing competition outfit.

Sharon
> What happened?

Kim
> Well, I was entertaining the whole of software. I had them eating putty out of my hands. It was going so well, when stupid Brett made me fall off my clacky mules. I sat on a seven thousand dollar plasma screen TV.

Sharon
> Oh, so he didn't get his promotion, then?

Kim
> No. But I'm rapt to the back teeth. I tell you what, Sharon, being a corporate wife is such a thankless task. I'm not just some man's crutch. Nuh. I'm going to concentrate on my own career.

Sharon
> Well, that's great, Kim.

Kim
> Yeah.

Sharon
> What are you going to be?

Kim
> A trophy wife.

Sharon
> Oh. What do they do?

Kim
> Nothing. And that's my pacific skill base. They just sit around looking beautiful.

Sharon
> Oh, thereby making their husbands look more powerful.

Kim
> That's right. Yeah.

Sharon
> Yeah.

Kim
> Yep. Fergie. Anna-Nicole Smith. Big shoes to fill.

Scene 18 Exterior – Kath's house – Day

Kel and Kath are walking through the front door with their bags.

Kel
Here we are. Home, sweet home.

Kath looks at herself in the mirror. So does Kel. We see their surgery.

Scene 19 Interior – Kath's house *(Good room)* – Day

Kel
Ohh!

Kath
Oh, I feel like a new woman, Kel!

Kel
Oh, so do I, but where are we gonna find one this time of night.

Kath
Oh, Kel. If you did your hair Chewbacca style, you could make a very respectable John Laws.

Kel
Oh, thank you very much.

Kath
No, I feel sensational.

Kel
Oh, you certainly do. Come here, you.

Kath
Oh no, no, no, stop Kel. We've got to get to Sharon's river dancing. I think it starts about eight. Her first time.

Kel
Come on! House to ourselves.

Kath
Oh no, Kel. No. Ohh! Ohh! Back in business, eh?

Kel
>Oh, I reckon.

Kath
>Oh, that feels nice. What do you call that?

Kel
>That's my botox.

Scene 20 Interior – Molly Bloom's pub – Night

At the hall where the Irish-dancing competition is being held, we see Mark smiling broadly at the lovely, leggy Moira dancing. Kath and Kel sit next to Kim and Brett. Kel is sitting – not talking, looking sheepish and upset.

Kath
>Oh come on, Kel. It's alright. Doesn't matter. It'll come back.

Kel
>Nuh. Now I'm worried. As the wise man once said, 'I think I've lost my mojo'.

Kath
>Oh Kel, stop it. We can go to the doctor and get some Viagra or something. Have a piece of bread and enjoy the night.

Kim
>Give us a look. Oh my God!

Kath
>What?

Kim
>It looks really good. Looks really subtle.

Kath
>Well you know, Kim, these days, frankly, I don't think you can get by without a little bit of work, really.

Kim
>No, it's very common.

Kath
> Yeah, it is common.

Kim
> It's common.

Kath
> It's ...

Kim
> It's nice. It's unusual.

Kath
> It's nice. It's unusual.

Kim
> It's common.

Kath
> And you ... you know, everyone I know's doing it. Liz, Michael, Melanie Griffiths.

Kim
> Well she looks a hundred bucks.

Kath
> She does.

Kim
> Brett, can I've a drink?

Kim
> Hello! Trophy wife in need of a cardonnay!

Kath
> Shh! Sharon's on next, Kim.

Mark
> Contestant two. Sharon Strezlecki.

Sharon comes on to the stage. Moira comes back on. Sharon muscles her off the stage. Kath, Kel, Kim and Brett are sitting at the table. Sharon is a hit with the audience. Sharon runs up to the table as they all clap.

Brett
> Hey, Shaz!

Sharon
>Gee, Mrs. D. You look really different. Have you done something to your hair?

Kath
>No, Sharon. Just been on a nice relaxing holiday. What about you up there? And Mark?

Sharon
>Oh, I don't care about him anymore, Mrs. D. No, I've discovered that developing an interest in a really sexy, sensual form of dance like Irish dancing is the perfect outlet for all my urges. So I've practically done away with men altogether, actually.

Mark
>I really liked your dancing.

Sharon
>Did you really?

Sharon and Mark have a moment, and then they start to pash.

Mark
>Official duties.

There is an announcement over the loudspeaker.

Mark
>Ah, and now it's time for the forties and over.

Kath
>Oh. Come on, Kel. Come and trip the light fandango with the lady of the dance. Come on.

Brett
>Go, Kath! Go Kel!

Brett
>Hey, Mrs. D!

It is Kath and Kel's turn. They dance wildly. Suddenly Kel feels something he hasn't felt for a while and pushes Kath over.

Kath
>Kel, what are you doing?

Kath
    Kel!

Kel riverdances lying on Kath.

Scene 21 Exterior – Kath's house/backyard – Day

Kim is reading her magazine. Kath comes with her drink.

Kath
    The sun's trying to break through.

Kim
    Oh, are you having a savignon plonk?

Kath
    Yes.

Kim
    Yum.

Kath
    Mm.

Kim
    Do you know what I really miss, Mum? Going to the pub and getting literally legless.

Kath
    Yeah. Gee, the other night was a nice night though, wasn't it, Kim?

Kim
    Yeah, it was. It was. Sharon really found her feet with the river dancing, didn't she?

Kath
    Oh. Kel's found more than just his feet.

Kim
    Mum!

Kath

Mm. I still think it was pretty unfair, though. I mean, we should have won that comp. Where does it say in the rule book that horizontal river dancing isn't part of the code?

Kim

Oh I tell you what, the audience got more than they bargained for, that's for sure.

Kath

Well now Kel's back on the carbs, he wants me to go river dancing every five minutes, if you get my drift.

Kim

Yes, I get it loud and revoltingly clear. And Mum, your face looks all normal again. What happened to the surgery?

Kath

No Kim, it wasn't surgery. It was non-invasive 'erbal. It was only designed to last a few days.

Kim

Well what a waste of money.

Kath

Oh no it wasn't, Kim. It was just an expensive learning curve. And I think it was worth it.

Kim

Oh, Mum. You know when Rachel in 'Friends' had her baby? She just had the cutest little bump. I think I'm going to be like that.

Kath

Oh Kim, that wasn't real. That was just Jennifer Anniston with a pillow stuffed up her jumper.

Kim

Oh, really? Well how come she's got a baby in the show now?

Kath

Oh God, you're stupid. I mean, for a girl who's done Stott Secretarial, you're very slow on the uptake, Kim. Actually, you didn't finish that course, did you?

Kim
No.

Kath
Maybe that's why.

Kim
I finished my cake decorating course though, thank you.

Kath
Oh, just. With a little help from Sara Lee.

Kel
Kath!

Kath
Oh, here we go.

Kel
Kath!

Kath
Coming, Kel.

Kim
Rather you than me.

Kath
Quick, hide the fags.

My Boyfriend 5

* Kim and Brett go furniture shopping
* Brett doesn't think he is manly enough
* Sharon ropes in everybody for her netball semi-final
* Kath is doing a TAFE Flower Arranging Course
* Kath's telephone breaks – she waits for Telstra
* Sharon gets to know her boyfriend

Scene 1   Interior – Ikea – Day

Kim and Brett are shopping at Ikea. They're deciding on change tables. Kim is staring love eyes at Brett.

Kim
No, Brett. You listen to me for once. I am rapt in you, mister.

Brett
What?

Kim
You're the man. It's your call.

Brett
Oh, I don't know anything about change tables.

Kim
You know everything. Come on, decide. The Ingmar or the Ullman?

Brett
Oh, that's a lot of pressure, Kim. You decide. You usually do.

Kim
But I'm pregnant you now, Brettie. I'm going to rely really heavily on you.

Brett
Yeah, what if I get it wrong and you go ballistic at me?

Kim
As if! You're funny. I'm going to cook your favourite tea tonight. Rack off lamb. Oh look Brett, there's the ball room. You know, the creche? When the baby's born, it's going straight in there. You can leave them in there all day, for free.

Brett
You're gonna make a top mum, Kim.

Kim
I need to go to the toot.

Brett
Alright. I'll wait here.

Kim
Oh, will you? Will you, just?

Man
Move it, mate.

Brett gets pushed along.

Brett
Oh, um, yeah.

Man
Follow the arrows.

Brett
Yeah, sorry. But I'm ... I'm waiting.
My wife. She's, ah ...

Man
There's no going back. You've got to go forward.

Brett
Kim!

Brett gets pushed further along.

Brett
Kim!

Kim goes to the toilet. We see a bathroom behind her. She goes to the toilet. Cut to reveal that the bathroom is only a display. Two sales assistants move bathroom display wall revealing Kim on the loo.

Kim *(voiceover)*
Where's the toilet paper? I'm not using that bidet.

Brett
Kim!

Kim comes out of toilet display.

Kim
Brett! Bretty!

Scene 2 Exterior – Kath's house – Day

Kath
Don't touch it, Kel. It'll go brown.

Kath is working on a flower hat. Kel has the hat on.

Kel
I reckon this suits me.

Kath
Stop moving. Keep still. I just ... I just want it to look a little bit like what Catherine Zeta wore when she married Michael Douglas.

Kel
I think you need some arum lilies, you know, at the back, to give it some height.

Kath
No, Kel, not arum lilies. They're so funereal, I feel. Now what does it need? It's coming to me. It's coming. I know, aspersions, yes.

Kel
You reckon, Kath?

Kath
Yeah.

Kath moves around Kel and picks up flower to place on hat.

Kath
I've got the inkstinks for floral design, Kel.

Kel
I guess you know.

Kath
Yes. Leave it there.

Kel
How's that look?

Kath
Oh!

Kath pulls flowers from hat.

Kath
No, don't like it. Hopeless, Kath.

Scene 3 Interior – Ikea *(Various sections)* – Day

Kim is walking through Ikea looking for Brett.

Kim
Brettie!

Kim *(voiceover)*
Now I'm in my second trimester, the happy hormones have really kicked in.

Woman with pram is blocking her way.

Kim
Move the pram, dickhead!

Woman
Oh, sorry.

My Boyfriend

Kim *(voiceover)*
> I'm feeling like a big, contented cow and I have to say, the sun is shining right out of Brett. He's so gorgeous, so strong, so brave.

Brett is lost at Ikea. He is sweating and on the verge of a panic attack.

Scene 4   Interior – Kath's house *(Livingroom)* – Day

Kel appears around corner wearing a hat. Kath is working on her computer.

Kel
> It looks fine, Kath.

Kath
> Fine isn't good enough. It's gotta be perfect! This is my final floral design piece. My assessment piece.

Kel
> Oh come on, it's just flowers.

Kath
> Flowers! You don't realise, this TAFE course I am doing in floral design, Kel, is the most penultimate course you can do in the country. And it's insane in there. I'm just getting so stressed.

Kel
> Oh, come on, Kath. Just relax. How about a bit of afternoon delight? I can leave my hat on.

Kath
> Oh no, Kel! Oh, I've gotta study.

Kel
> Alright. I know when I'm not wanted. I might choof off down to Umpire's World and picks up a few supplies for the Unicorns' big game this afternoon. You haven't forgotten, have ya?

Kath
> No, I haven't forgotten. It's just another thing I've gotta do. I've just got to learn to say no.

Kel
>Well, see you courtside. I'm going to take your phone. Mine's dead.

Kath
>Start again. Right. Kath, okay. Take one mini-cowboy hat, to which I add one green foam block.

Scene 5 Interior – Ikea – Day

Ikea staff member
>Attention, please. We have a lost child in the store.

Kim leans down to the microphone

Kim
>Here I'll do it. Um, hello. If anyone has seen a little fellow wearing a Piping Hot top and Hot Tuna cargo shorts. He's about six foot three and answers to the name of Brett. Could you please bring him to the ball room immediately. Thank you.

Scene 6 Interior – Kath's house *(Livingroom)* – Day

Kath is studying on computer

Kath
>That's it. Gypsophila Paniculata. Baby's breath! That is the key. Oh, but it's not in flower. Just my luck! Hey! What's going on? What's happened?

The computer is playing up. Sharon enters. Kath hardly listens to Sharon.

Sharon
>Hi, Mrs. D. Is Kimmy here? I've got her netball uniform.

Kath
>Oh, bloody computers! Oh, what?

Sharon
>Did I tell you, Mrs. D? Ah, my boyfriend, Mark, is going to come and watch me play for the first time this arvo.

Kath
> What, Sharon?

Sharon
> My boyfriend. Oh, you haven't forgotten, Mrs. D? It's the mixed team semi. I've got you playing wing attack.

Kath
> No, I haven't forgotten, Sharon. But, you know, netball's a game. Floral design could be my life's work, my chicken feed. And I've got to get my piece finished.

Sharon
> My boyfriend is artistic.

Kath
> And I tell you, I am pushing the proverbial uphill. You know, there are some people there who have done degrees at CAE, for God's sake. You know, they're doing amazing things with kangaroos paws and lamb's ears. What have I got?

Sharon
> Okay, I'll leave you to it, then. If you see Kim, can you tell her that I'll just be with my boyfriend? Ta ta.

Kath
> Gypsophila Paniculata.

Scene 7   Interior – Ikea parcel pick up – Day

Brett and Kim are waiting for their stuff at parcel pickup. Kim is sitting on Brett's lap.

Kim
> Well, where were you, Brett? I was really worried about you.

Brett
> Oh, I got lost. I just freaked out a bit, that's all.

Kim
> Well how can I rely on you to look after bubs and me if you get lost in a furniture shop?

Brett
>Oh come on, Kim. It's the biggest store in the southern hemisphere.

Kim
>I need you to be the man.

Brett
>What does that mean?

Kim
>I don't know. Be good with directions. Know how to use an allen key. Stuff like that.

Brett
>Can you get up, Kim? You're really heavy.

Ikea man comes with some flat packs.

Man
>There's your Ingmar and Bergman.

Brett
>No, we ordered a cot and a change table.

Man
>You've gotta put it together yourself, mate.

Brett
>What? I have to build it?

Kim
>Yes.

Brett struggles with the parcels.

Brett
>Have you got a trolley?

Kim
>Oh, you can carry it, Brett. Come on, big strong muscles.

Scene 8   Interior – Mark's flat – Day

Sharon
So anyway, my tracky dacks got caught in the chain, and I went A over T, right over the handlebars. My arm was cactus. Five weeks in plaster.

Mark
You know, the same thing happened to me, only I broke my humorous and my cartilage, and the doctor said it was the worst greenstick injury she'd ever seen.

Sharon
Wow. 'Course, mine was quite complicated, you know, 'cause it was in the outback, and it was three hours to the nearest hospital.

Mark
Yeah, well mine was in Thailand, and they don't have hospitals there, so I had to set it myself. And the doctor said it was the best job they'd ever seen.

Sharon
Oh, wow. Gee you know, Mark, I really wish you could play with us today. Mixed netball's so much fun, you know? The guys and the girls together.

Mark
You know, I would like to help, and I am a very good player, but fiddle hands.

Sharon
Yeah. 'Course. Well, the Unicorns are a really strong team you know. We've got Mrs. D, and Kim. Kel's umpiring.

Mark starts to play his fiddle.

Mark
Shh. Listen.

Sharon
Sorry, Mark.

Sharon starts to clap.

Mark
>No, you're out of time.
>Two, three, four.

Scene 9   Interior – Brett and Kim's unit – Day

Brett is in the nursery. He is reading the Ikea instructions.

Brett
>Then hammer dowls one oh one, three five eight, and one oh one, three five one, in place. What? How does that work?

Kim comes in.

Kim
>Hi, you.

Brett
>Hi. What?

Kim
>Nothing. Hello. How's it going?

Brett
>I don't think I can put this cot together. I don't even understand the instructions.

Kim
>'Course you can put it together. You have to. That's what guys do. It's nice. It's normal.

Brett
>Maybe I'm not normal.

Kim
>Just put it up, Brett. I'm going to Mum's to get my netball uniform.

Scene 10   Interior – Kath's house *(Kitchen/livingroom)* – Day

Kim
Mum!

Kath
In the good room. Where does that go? What are the lines doing here?

Kim
Has Sharon left my netball uniform here? 'Cause she says I'm not allowed to play if I don't wear it.

Kath
It's there on the table. Oh, I give up. I tell you, Kimmy, my brain is fried.

Kim
Mum, I'm seriously doubting Brett's ability to provide for his growing family.

Kath
What? What's your beef today?

Kim
Well, do you think Brett's manly?

Kath
'Course he's manly, Kim. Look how good he is with computers.

Kim
Well some girls are good at computers, too.

Kath
Not this little black duck.

Kim
I've just got this little niggly feeling that maybe, you know, he's a complete dud.

Kath
You could do a lot worse, Kim.

Kim

Well, he doesn't mow the lawn, he can't build anything, he can't fix the car. I mean, seriously, Mum, what if we were on Survivor? We'd be voted off after the first week.

Kath

Kimmy. Kimmy, look at me, please. Look at me. Look at me. Now I've got one word to say to you, Kim. Thinking woman's crumpet.

Kim

What?

Kath

Well Brett's a modern guy. Get with the program. He doesn't need to do all that stuff. That's why we invented whitegoods and Jim's Mowing.

Scene 11   Interior – Mark's house – Day

Sharon

Oh Mark, I've heard you play so many times. I never get sick of it.

Mark

Well, I come alive in front of an audience.

Sharon

And today's your chance to see me doing what I do best.

Mark

And I am looking forward to seeing you in your little netball outfit.

Sharon

Oh. Oh my God, look at the time. I've gotta get to the court. I'm going to have to really gun it. Lucky I'm a top driver.

Mark

Hey, I used to be the Victorian rally car champ, so don't talk to me about top driving.

Scene 12 Interior – Kath's house *(Kitchen/livingroom)* – Day

Kath *(on phone)*
What? Oh, no. Oh, right. Thank you. Yes, bye. *(Kath hangs up)* Oh, it's a bloody disaster.

Kim
What's happened?

Kath
A statewide shortage of baby's breath, Kim.

Kim
What's that got to do with the price of Tia Maria?

Kath
My final floral design piece, Kim. The exhibition's tonight. I need baby's breath.

Kim
Well, calm down. Just think rashly. What else could you use? What about fruit?

Kath
No, I can't use fruit, Kim. It's a hat arrangement. I've got to model it. I'll look like Carmen Miranda Otto, or whatever her name is.

Kim
Mm, it's just a suggestion.

Kath
Well it's a stupid suggestion, alright?

Kim
Oh, whatever.

Phone rings. Kath answers.

Kath
Yes, hello? Yes, Coral. Yes. Alright, I'll just check on that. What was it?

Kim *(voiceover)*
Poor Mum. She's really going starkers. I might have a useless husband, but at least I'm not doing a course. I just feel for her so much. You know, I couldn't care more about Mum's final floral exam. I certainly couldn't care less.

Kath
Like Walt Disney? In a tube, yes. Okay, well I'll sit by the phone and wait. Okay, great. Thanks, Coral. *(She hangs up and puts the phone on the couch)* Oh, well that's good news, Kim. You wouldn't believe it. Apricot Flowers have sourced some baby's breath from the Gold Coast, and they're going to cryogenically freeze it for me and get it on the plane asap today.

Kim
You see, Mum? Don't sweat the small stuff. Take a chill pill.

Kim sits down on the couch.

Kath
Yes, I might just do that. I mean, my nerves are so bojangled at the moment. I had some 'erbal relaxants here somewhere. *(Kath finds them and takes one)* Yes. I'd better call Kel. Tell him the good news. Mm, where's the phone, Kim? What have I done with the phone?

Kim
Oh, I don't know.

Kath
I'll have to page it.

Kath pushes the 'page' button. Kim is sitting on the phone. We hear a muffled beeping.

Kath
It's over there near you, Kim.

Kim leans over to look for the phone. The beeping becomes louder.

Kim
Nuh.

Kim bends over again.

Kath
> Yes. Oh. You're sitting on it, Kim.

Kim
> Ooh.

Kath
> Fool.
> Oh, it's buggered. It's all fuzzy now, Kim. And I wanted to hear from Coral!

Kath checks the phone. It doesn't work. Kim takes phone.

Kim
> Oh, give it to me. You know, I did work in a Call Centre. I do know about phones.

Kim bashes the phone a few times.

Kim
> There you go.

Kath
> Thank you. Oh, it's completely dead now, Kim.

Kim
> Oh, well I didn't do it.

Kath
> Well, you know, I'll have to call Telstra. The computer's down, the phone's gone. I'll use your mobile. Kel's got mine. Hello? Put me on hold. One for lines down. Two for external. I don't know what it is. Greensleeves. Oh yes, hello, Trish? Yes. Yes, it's Kath Day-Knight. Um, yeah, look, my phone lines are down, or there's something wrong with the phones, and I need to be urgently contactable by my local florist at present. All day. Well can you narrow down the time a bit, please? Alright. Thank you, Trish.

Kim
> Alright, I'd better go. I've got to go and pick up Brett, and I'll, ah, see you at the courts.

Kim takes her phone and leaves. Kath is annoyed.

Kath
> Oh, don't take that, Kim. I need it.

Kim
> No, I need it!

Kath
> Well what am I going to do? I've got to wait here for Telstra all day? Alright, I'll see you there later. I'll be there.

Kath takes another tablet.

Scene 13 Interior – Netball court – Day

Sharon hands out the bibs to the team members.

Sharon
> Ashley.

Brett
> Why aren't you on the team today? Sharon reckons you're a bit of a gun.

Mark
> Oh, don't play amateur, mate. Not fair on the other team. Besides, netball, bit of a girls' sport. Speaking of which ... *(Woman walks left to join rest of team)*

Mark
> What about you? You playing?

Brett
> Oh, no. No, no good at sport, mate. No talent in that area. Happy to watch. My wife Kim plays. She's having a baby, actually.

Mark
> Is she? Yeah, I nearly had a baby once. Turned out the girl wasn't pregnant.

He pulls out the Ikea instructions

Brett
> You seem pretty good at everything, mate. Hey, ah, can you understand this?

Mark
> Oh yeah, yeah. Yeah, I lived in Sweden for five years. Ootan haffen norgan vargen.

Scene 14   Interior – Netball court – Day

Sharon and the team are warming up. Sharon is showing off for Mark's benefit

Sharon
> Nice! Now you're workin', now you're workin'. That it! Faster! Nice work. Kimmy, what are you doing? This is important! Concentrate!

Kim
> Huh?

Sharon
> Kimmy!

Sharon slaps Kim across face.

Kim
> Ow!

Sharon
> Hi, Mark.

She waves to Mark, but he ignores her talking to Brett.

Mark
> See, it's a bit of a line? That's ... that's my way.

Sharon
> Hi, Mark.

Mark
> That's not necessarily how ...

Sharon
That's, ah, that's my boyfriend.

Kel enters. He has his umpire's uniform on: white shorty shorts and top and a whistle. He blows the whistle.

Kel
Five minutes! Five minutes. Nails please.

Kel walks past players inspecting fingernails then Sharon moves to him.

Sharon
Kel, Kel. We can't. Mrs. D isn't here yet.

Kel
Five minutes.

Sharon
Well, where can she be?

Scene 15 Interior – Kath's house *(Kitchen/livingroom)* – Day

---

A slightly chilled Kath is busy making her arrangement. It is an odd mix of flowers with fruit.

Kath
Oh, I'm going to be stuck here all day waiting for Telstra.

There is a pineapple on the table.

Kath
I'll take the pineapple. The chopsticks in the pineapple.

Kath holds up pineapple.

Kath
Hey, I like what I see. Yeah. Who needs silly old baby's breath when I've got this beautiful Yepoon pineapple?

Kath thinks she hears a knock at the front door.

Kath
Must be Telstra. Hm, that's quick.

Scene 16   Exterior/Interior – Kath's house/entrance – Day

Kath opens door. No-one is there.

> **Kath**
>> Oh. Going mad. Maybe I shouldn't have taken that second chill pill. There's somewhere I was s'posed to be today.

Scene 17   Interior – Netball court – Day

The game is yet to start. The teams are waiting. It is tense. Sharon is talking to Mark.

> **Sharon**
>> Oh please, Mark. You yourself said you're a fantastic player. Oh, please. We'll be disqualified if we don't have a full team. Please.
>
> **Mark**
>> Yeah. Yeah, yeah alright Sharon. Sure.
>
> **Sharon**
>> Oh, great. Quick, we've just got one spare uniform.
>
> **Mark**
>> My pleasure.
>
> **Sharon**
>> Everyone! It's okay. My boyfriend is gonna play.
>
> **Mark**
>> Watch and weep, Brett.

Scene 18   Interior – Kath's house *(Shower)* – Day

> **Kath *(voiceover)***
>> Oh, look at the fluff in the fan. That's shocking.

Kath thinks she hears someone at the front door again.

Kath
> Oh, that's the door. Oh, no! Telstra, Telstra, I'm coming!

Scene 19 Exterior – Kath's *(Front garden/street)* – Day

Kath wanders outside in a daze with just a towel on. She is in the front garden.

Kath
> Telstra. Oh, bloody pigs!

Kath picks up rubbish then looks through the bag of rubbish and takes out chopsticks.

Kath
> Oh, more chopsticks. Oh, they're nice. Unusual.

There is a neighbour in the garden.

Kath
> Oh, hello.

Kath opens towel.

Kath
> Yes, I am woman, see me roar. I'm waiting for Telstra, actually, if it's any of your bee's wax.

Scene 20 Interior – Netball court – Day

Sharon runs around on court with others nearby. Brett is watching. The game is underway. Kel is umpiring. Mark is chatting up his opposing player.

Sharon
> If you need. If you need!

Mark
> I am a muso by trade, and ah, single by nature.

Mark's opponent throws the ball and the other team goals.

Sharon
> Come on. Come on, Eunuchs! What was that, Mark? What are you doing? If you need!

Someone throws Mark the ball, it whizzes past him he stumbles. Sharon is dumbfounded and increasingly pissed off. An opposing player crowds in on Kim.

Player
> Oh, out of the way, fatty.

Kim
> Oh, obstruction! She can't speak to me like that! I'm pregnant!

The other umpire blows the whistle.

Umpire
> You're in the breach of the rules and must leave the court.

Kim
> That is so backward. Being pregnant has had absolutely no effect on my playing skills.

Sharon
> That's right. She was shocking even before she was pregnant.

Kim
> Kel! Help me, please?

Kel
> Off!

The siren goes for half-time.

Scene 21   Interior – Netball court – Day

Sharon is devastated.

Sharon
> This is not fair. I can't believe it. We're so close. What are we going to do?

My Boyfriend

Kim
>Brett, you've gotta play.

Brett
>Oh, oh I can't, Kim. I'm hopeless.

Sharon
>There's no point, anyway. We don't have any uniforms. Oh, we're going to be disqualified.

Brett
>Honestly Kim, I'm no good.

Kim
>Well, you're no good at millions of things but you still do them. What kind of man are you, Brett!

Brett
>Kim! Kim! Kim.

Scene 22 Interior – Netball court – Day

Kim
>That's my husband. In the dress. Whoo hoo! Go, Brett.

Sharon
>Brett! Brettie! Brett!

Brett comes onto the court in Kim's uniform. It is a skirt and top. He starts to play. He is really good. Sharon has the ball.

Brett
>If you need ...
>Inside, inside!

Brett passes the ball and their team goals. Brett and Sharon high five. A player throws ball then Brett intercepts. Sharon cheers. Brett scores goal, pulls the bib over his face, and runs around.

Kim
>You're a hornbag, Brett!

Scene 23 Interior – Netball court – Day

The siren goes and they all rejoice. Kim is all over Brett.

Kim
Brett. I'm feeling a lot of feelings. I'm sorry I doubted you.

Brett
Were you doubting me, Kim? I would never have noticed.

Kim
I don't care if you can't put up a change table. It can rot in hell as far as I'm concerned.

Brett
It's already up. I rang Dial-A-Hubby, put it up in ten minutes, job done.

Kel
Well done, Brett.

Brett
Yeah, thanks, Kel.

Kel
Mm, just watch your stepping.

Brett
Yeah, sure.

Kim
Wonder what happened to Mum?

Kel
Oh, I guess she was up to her armpits in pussy willow and clean forgot. Her exhibition's in an hour, so she's probably frantic.

Scene 24 Interior – Kath's house *(Livingroom)* – Day

Kath is asleep on the couch.

> **Kath**
> Oh! Oh, I've gotta go! The exhibition! What's the time? Oh!

Scene 25 Interior – Netball court – Day

> **Sharon**
> What'd you think you were doing, Mark? This is the second semi-final! You told me you could play. You lied to me.
>
> **Mark**
> I didn't lie. I embellished. That's what I do. I'm an artist. Oh, Sharon. Now come on. It's just a game.
>
> **Sharon**
> I beg your pardon?
>
> **Mark**
> It's just a bit of hit and giggle with the girls.
>
> **Sharon**
> That's it, Mark. No boyfriend of mine denigrates the code and gets away with it. It's over.

Kim and Brett approach protectively, and Mark leaves.

> **Kim**
> You alright, Sharon?
>
> **Sharon**
> Yeah, I just got something in my eye.
>
> **Kim**
> Oh, don't worry. One day you'll meet a real macho man like Brett.

Scene 26 Interior – Kath's house *(Good room)* – Night

Kim, Kath, Kel, Sharon and Brett are sitting around after the exhibition having a Baileys. The hat is sitting pride of place with a blue first prize ribbon. There is a sign reads 'Waiting for Telstra ... An Absurdist Piece'.

Kim
> Alright, everybody. Everybody. Bit of shoosh. I want to propose a toast. To someone who is not only a huge spunk rat, but is also the biggest hottie in Fountain Lakes. Me. For having the smarts to choose a husband like Brett.

Brett
> Oh thanks, Kim.

Kim
> No, don't. I haven't finished yet. Oh, I've forgotten what I was going to say, Brett! Oh, I've gotta go to the toot.

Kath
> Oh, I think those happy hormones are finally leaving.

Brett
> Thank God.

Kel stands to propose toast.

Kel
> I would also like to propose a toast to Kath, the foxiest florist ...

Kath
> Uh-uh! Floral designer, please.

Kel
> ... floral designer this side of Fountain Lakes. Yes, Kath has taken out first prize for her absurdist piece, 'Waiting For Telstra'. To Kath.

Sharon and Brett
> Mrs. D.

Kath
> Thank you.

Sharon is looking quiet. The microwave dings.

Brett
>I'll get the footy franks, Sharon. Don't worry. Better check Chuckles.

Sharon
>So, um, where do you get your ideas, Mrs. D?

Kath
>Oh, well thank you for asking, Sharon. Yes, well you know, I just take scenarios from my daily life, ah, vis a vie, ah, waiting for Telstra to turn up, um, the fluff from the shower fan, and …

Kel
>The pineapple was inspired.

Kath
>Oh yes. Well look, that just hit me when I opened the fridge. Literally. Oh, what's that?

We hear the sad sound of the fiddle outside the window playing 'What about me?' slowly.

Sharon
>Oh, don't worry. It's just Mark out in the foliage again.

Kath
>Oh well, do you want me to ask him in? Do you want to see him?

Sharon
>Oh, no. No, Mrs. D. He's my ex-boyfriend now.

Kath
>Oh. And how are you with that, Sharon? You know, deep within yourself?

Sharon
>Oh, couldn't be happier, Mrs D. I'm a Eunuch, and that makes me proud.

Kath
>Oh.

Kel
> The Eunuchs.

Sharon
> To Eunuchs.

Kath
> To Eunuchs, yes. Of course.

Scene 27　Exterior – Kath's house *(Backyard)* – Day

Kath
> Oh, it's depressing. There's nothing on telly at the moment.

Kim
> Wheel of Fortune's on.

Kath
> Oh, Wheel hasn't been the same since Adrianna Obsenides left.

Kim
> Did you see that 'Search For An Idol'? Did you see the people they picked?

Kath
> Mm.

Kim
> I mean, why didn't they choose me? I am so idle.

Kath
> You said it. I.D.L.E.

Kim
> Mum!

Kath
> Far And Away's on, with Tom and Nicole. I do like that.

Kim
> Oh, so do I. Do you know what gets up my goat? Why don't they ever put Nicole on the cover of a magazine? I mean, what's that about?

Kath
> Oh Kim, it's the tall poppy syndrome. You know, I've been a victim of that ever since I won my award.

Kim
> Oh yes. How, pacifically?

Kath
> Well, the whole floral design department is green. I mean, some little B put in a protest because apparently a pineapple isn't strictly a flower. Well hello, I think a whole lot of spanner clutching's going on.

There is a knock at the door.

Telstra man
> Hello, Telstra!

Kim
> Oh, I'll get it.

Kath
> No, Kim. Don't. Let 'em wait.

Telstra man
> Hello! Anyone home? Telstra!

Kim
> Mum!

Kath
> No, Kim. Just sit there. Give him a taste of his own medicine. I'm not going to get up. Bugger him.

Another Announcement

- Sharon auditions to be a Commonwealth Games Volunteer
- Brett goes out in sympathy
- Kim goes to labour class
- Kath and Kel decide to have a new addition to the family
- Kel reveals his past donations

Scene 1 Interior – Fountain Gate Mall – Day

Kath and Kim are shopping at Fountain Gate Mall.

> **Kath**
> Oh, I'm so exhausted now I'm carrying, Kim.
>
> **Kim**
> What?
>
> **Kath**
> Now I'm carrying all the shopping.

Kath is carrying heaps of bags.

> **Kim**
> Oh.
>
> **Kath**
> I have forgotten, though. It's so exciting, isn't it? It's so much fun. We haven't got a lot of time, though.
>
> **Kim**
> Oh, hello! Who's having this baby?

They go past a baby shop.

> **Kath**
> Oh, Kimmy, look! The nautical look. That's so cute.

Kim
>Ohhhh!

Kath
>It's so cute.

Kim
>Nautical look. It's nice. It's so nice.

Kath
>It is nice. It's different. It's unusual.

Kim
>It's different.

Kim and Kath *(in unison)*
>It's unusual.

Kath
>It is nice. It's different.

Kim
>It is so cute.

Kath
>It is different.

Kim
>Look at the little bow tie!

Kath
>Yeah. Oh, but Kimmy, I've done all the shopping for the baby. You know, your layette and such. So we just need to finish off for you.

Kim
>Mmm ...

Kath
>So, let's do a quick itinerary. What do we need to get?

Kim
>And the Hooley Dooley breast pump and sponge bag.

Kath
>Check.

Kim
> And the Wiggles maxi-pads.

Kath
> Check. So that just leaves the Bob the Builder nipple guards to get, Kim.

Kim
> Yep.

Kath
> Oh, that's done.

Kath
> I tell you, Kim, I could kill for a chino.

Kim
> Have a mug of chino.

Kath
> Oh no, that's too big. I don't like mugs.

Scene 2 Interior – Fountain Gate Mall *(Food court)* – Day

Kath and Kim are sitting having a coffee.

Kim
> Ooh, and I've got to go and get my bean bag.

Kath
> Kim.

Kim
> What?

Kim has froth on her upper lip.

Kim
> Oh.

Kath
> So is Brettie excited about going to birth classes this arvo?

Another Announcement

Kim
> No, he doesn't even want to come. Anyway, he'll be hopeless at the birth. He was no use at the conception.

Kath
> Don't be stupid, Kim. What do you mean, he was no use at the conception?

Kim
> All I'm saying is, I had to do everything myself, as per usual.

Kath
> And can you leave off my Tira Misu, please?

Kim
> Gee Tirama Sue. That's a pretty name.

Kath
> It is, Kim.

Kim and Kath *(in unison)*
> Tirama Sue.

Kath
> Make a mental note, Kath. Remember name.

Kim
> Alright, I'd better go.

Kath
> Oh Kim, those Bumsters, they're splitting already.

Kim
> Mum, they're maternity Bumsters. They're meant to split. It's the look. Anyway, I've gotta go to Target. Get my bean bag for birth classes.

Kath notices Kim's thighs.

Kath
> Speaking of bean bags.

Kim
> What?

Another Announcement

Kath
> Your thighs. I mean, cottage cheese is nice, love, but not on your legs.

Kim
> Give it a bone, Mum.

Kim leaves.

Kath
> Kim, don't forget ...

Kim
> What?

Kath
> Kel and I are going to choose your pram today.

Kim
> Yes, I know.

Kath
> So can I see you back in the Barina in ten minutes, please?

Kim
> Yeah, alright.

Kath
> We're in P2, Kim.

Kath sees a baby in a pram, the father is nearby.

Kath
> Oh, look at the eyes. What a wise little face. He's been here before, hasn't he?

Father
> He's a girl.

Scene 3   Exterior – Brett's car/Hospital entrance – Day

Brett
> What's wrong with the name Murray?

Another Announcement

Kim
> It's foul.

Brett
> It's my Dad's name.

Kim
> Says it all. Brett, why can't you compromise for once and just do what I say? Anyway, it's going to be a girl.

Brett
> Nuh, it's a boy. 'Cause they say when you have a boy you look sort of square, like a tank, from the bank.

Kim
> Like a tank? You're really getting up my goat today, Brett. Where are you going? The hospital's over that way

Brett
> Why do we even have to do birth classes?

Kim
> Because it's nice. It's normal.

Brett
> It's bloody embarrassing.

Kim
> Brett, what are you doing? This is the casualty entrance. You can't park here. There are ambliances coming up behind us. Just go down there.

Brett
> I can't! It's one way!

Kim
> Well it doesn't matter!

Brett
> Bloody hell!

Brett drives out. Kim sees a sign

Kim
> Brett! This is the wrong hospital, you idiot!

Brett
I'm goin' home.

We see the car screech around and drive off.

Scene 4   Exterior – Kath's house – Day

Kath and Kel are getting the Jogger three-wheeler pram out of Kath's car. Kel also unloads home brew gear (yeast etc.) and puts it in the garage.

Kath
Oh gee, it's light. So how do you get it up, Kel?

Kel
Just hang on. I'll get the instructions.

Kath
Oh, God. Maybe we should have got the umbarella style, Kel.

Kel
That goes into there. Just hang on. Push that out like that.

Kath
Right.

Kel
And ...

Kath
Oh, that's easy.

Kel
... bingo.

Kath
Gee, look at that. Oh, smooth. Gee, it'd be so easy to have a baby these days.

Scene 5   Interior/Exterior – Brett's car/Kath's house – Day

Brett and Kim are fighting.

Kim
Well, you're going next week and the week after that and the week after that until I say, and that's final, Brett.

Brett
You know, I should have a say in some things, Kim. It is my baby too, you know.

Kim
Don't get cocky.

Brett
What's that supposed to mean, Kim?

Kim looks around.

Scene 6 Interior – Kath's house *(Good room)* – Day

Kath is unpacking. Kel enters with a cot.

Kel
Right, that's the porta-cot. Oh, and the musical mobile. Plays a nice tune. Vulgar Boat Men.

Kath
Oh!

Kel hums tune.

Kath
That's pretty, isn't it Kel?

Kel
Yeah.

Kath
No, look, I do think it's easier for us to have our own nursery set up here.

Kel holds up baby outfit.

Kel
Something you want to tell me, love?

Kath

For Kim's baby. I mean, it's just easier for us to have our own set of everything.

Kel

You're not getting clucky, are you sweets?

Kath

Oh, no way, Jose. Been there, done that.

Kel holds up a Babygro.

Kel

Oh, have a look at that. So small, Kath.

Kath

Oh! Isn't that hysterical?

Scene 7   Interior – Kath's house *(Livingroom)* – Day

Kim and Brett barge in.

Brett

Yeah, well I s'pose we'd better get a DNA test, bettern we, Kim?

Kim

I was joking. You've got no sense of 'umour. Not like me. 'Course you're the father.

Brett

Well, you know I want to be involved as much as I can. It's just that I can't handle birth classes.

Kim

Well it's alright for you, isn't it? You don't have to carry it around, lose your beautiful figure and get fat.

Brett

I would if I could, Kim.

Kim

Oh, that is revolting, Brett. That is so –

Another Announcement

Kath
>Oh, time out! Time out, peoples! Time out!
>Now what's happening, Brett? What's your issue?

Brett
>Well I don't want to go to birth classes.

Kath
>And Kimmy, what's your beef?

Kim
>I don't want to call the baby Murray.

Kath
>Well alright, Brett. You don't have to go to birth classes, Kimmy, you don't have to call the baby Murray. Okay, we've got closure.

Kim
>Thanks, Mum.

Kath
>Good girl.

Brett
>Thanks for your commonsense, Mrs. D.

Kath
>No worries.

Kel
>Have a taste of this, Brett.

Brett
>Oh.

Kel
>It's my home brew.

Brett drinks the beer.

Brett
>Thanks, Kel

Kath
>Kimmy, come with me. I want to show you the pram.

Brett
> Yeah, that's good, mate.

Kel
> Actually, take a couple of bottles home. I'm more of a, ah, chardonnay man myself.

Brett drinks and does a burp.

Kel
> That's a compliment in some countries.

Scene 8 Interior – Kath's house *(Good room)* – Day

Kath can see Kel outside, painting the cot in a pair of stretch denims.

Kath *(voiceover)*
> Gee, Kel's right into this baby caper. I've got a hinkling he's got a secret yearning, you know. Maybe he wants a child. It is a waste. I mean, look at him. Genes to die for.

Kim
> What about these? Lourdes? Rocco? Paris? Prince? Blanket? Michael Jackson's called his kid Blanket. That's nice.

Kath
> Oh, there's some very pretty names around at the moment, Kim.

Kim
> Yeah.

Kath
> I've got Winona, Paloma, Papiloma.

Kim
> Oh, beautiful.

Kath
> That's nice. Yeah.

Kim
> Yeah.

Sharon enters wearing a uniform and a slouch hat.

Sharon
Hi, Mrs. D. Hi, Kim.

Kath
Hi, Sharon.

Kim
What have you come as?

Kath
Oh, don't you look dinki di!

Sharon
Yeah. Well I am just a bee's bit away from being an official Commonwealth Games volunteer.

Kath
Oh, Sharon, that's exciting.

Sharon
Yeah.

Kath
So what does that pacifically entail, love?

Sharon
Ah, well Mrs. D, given my sporting prowess, you know, like in netball and indoor cricket, I will be stationed outside the porta-loos motivating people to hurry up with the war cry, 'Aussie, Aussie, Aussie, oi, oi, oi!'

Kath
Oh well, you must feel terribly proud, Sharon.

Sharon
Yeah, I am, Mrs. D. Yeah, yeah. And it's just, you know, one little test away from being official.

Kath
Mm.

Sharon
Yeah. My lip's tingling. I hope I'm not getting a cold sore.

Kim
  Sharon, I've got something important to ask you.

Sharon
  Yes, Kim?

Kim
  Because you're my second best friend, and my husband is a dickhead, would you deign to come to birth classes with me?

Sharon
  I don't think I can, Kim.

Kim
  Yeah. Right.

Kim sulks.

Sharon
  Well, I mean, I have to check my games roster. I think I'm on call for training.

Kim
  Bloody hopeless, Sharon.

Sharon
  I am not hopeless, Kim! I am the official face of Melbourne! What about Tina?

Kim
  Oh, Tina is having her boob job reversed at the moment. You're such a fair weather second best friend, Sharon!!

Sharon
  I am not!

Kim
  You're unbelievable!

Sharon and Kim yell over top of each other.

Sharon
  You are my best friend!

Another Announcement

Kim
> You are not!

Sharon
> You know I am. You are! You don't care about –

Kim
> Okay, well I've decided—

Sharon
> – anything that I'm talking about!

Kim and Sharon
> – I'm not talking to you!

Kath
> Kimmy, Kimmy, Kimmy, Kimmy, look at me, please. Look at me. Look at me. Now I've got one word to say to you, Kim. Mifamwy.

Kim
> What?

Kath
> Mifamwy Kathleen Darleen Craig. For the baby. I think it's a beautiful name. So, can we settle on Mifamwy, can we?

Kim
> Mum, I am not having wee in my baby's name.

Kath
> Oh, well alright. Girls, can we have a pow-wow, please? Come on, sit down. I really want to get this name sorted out toot sweet, as of today. Come on.
> Right, now hit me with your suggies. Come on.

Sharon
> Right.

Kath
> Shoot.

Sharon
> I heard a really beautiful name the other day. Tailuh. T.a.i.l.u.h. Tailuh.

Kim
   Oh, that's nice.

Kath
   Tailuh, I like that. I'll write that down. T.a.i.l.u.h.

Kim
   I also really like Tiffany, Mum, spelt T.y.p.h.p.h.a.a.n.n.i.i.i. Isn't that nice?

Kath
   Oh, we'll put that down.

Kim
   It's a pretty spelling.

Kath
   Well I'll tell you another beautiful name that I happened upon was Eponnee-Rae, spelt E.p.p ... o.n.n. apostrophe nee.

Sharon
   Ah, Mrs. D, is that nee with a K?

Kath
   Yeah.

Sharon
   Oh.

Kath
   Um, R.a.e., Rae, umlaut, close italics.

Kim
   Eponnee-Rae.

Kath and Kim
   That's nice. It is.

Sharon
   That's nice.

Kath, Sharon and Kim speak over top of each other.

Sharon
   That is nice, Mrs. D. Um, but what if it's a boy?

Kath
> Oh, well I like old fashioned names, you know, like Victorian names. Glen Waverley. That's strong.

Kim
> No, no, no, it's going to be a girl. I can feel it in my waters.

Sharon
> Oh Kim, why don't we do the ring test?

Kim
> Oh yes, yes, yes, yes, yes!

Kath
> Oh, that's a good idea. Yeah, use your wedding ring.

Kim
> Alright, I'll go and lie on the couch.

Kath
> Yeah, go and lie on the touch. She does it over your tummy. Gives a very accurate reading, I find.

Sharon puts the ring on a string and hangs it over Kim's stomach.

Sharon
> Now if it goes round and round in a circle, then that means that it's a little girl, and if it goes up and down, it's going to be a boy.

Kim
> Yep, yep, come on.

Kath
> Oh, what happens if it goes from side to side? Look at that. Hey, dee, hey dee ho. I think it's an elephant, Kim.

Kim
> Oh, you're doing that yourself, Sharon. Oh Mum, everyone's mean to me. You're mean to me, Brett's mean to me, the baby's mean to me, kicking me when I'm down. Nobody cares.

Sharon
> I care, Kim.

Kim
> Do you, Sharon?

Sharon
> Come on, Kim. Buck up. Aussie, Aussie, Aussie, oi, oi, oi!

Kath
> Aussie. Now that's a nice name. Write that down.

Scene 9   Interior – Hall – Day

Sharon screws up form and begins writing again. Sharon turns to women seated nearby.

Sharon
> S.h.a.r. Excuse me, um, do you know where the ladies' toilet is, please?

Judge
> Next!

Scene 10   Interior – Hall/Judging Room – Day

Sharon walks across hall to a long table with a panel of judges conducting the audition.

Sharon
> Hi, I'm Sharon. Sharon Strezlecki. Very nice to meet you. Advance Australia Fair.

Sharon starts to sing

Sharon
> Australians all let us rejoice
> For we are young and free
> With golden ...

She starts to hum a bit as she doesn't know the words, gets confused, and by the end she is doing the Star-spangled Banner.

Sharon
> For the land of the brave.

Another Announcement

Scene 11 Interior – Kim and Brett's unit – Day

Kim is on the couch reading a book.

Kim
Nee Rae umlaut, close italics.

Brett
Oh, oh, I feel bad.

Brett enters the room with swollen belly.

Kim
Oh my God, Brett!

Brett
Something's happened to me, Kim.

Kim
What the hell are you doing?

Brett
I've heard about this. I've gone out in sympathy.

Kim
Oh, what are you saying? You're having a phantom pregnancy?

Brett
Oh, I don't know, Kim.

Kim
Well I do. You're stealing my thunder and I don't like it.

Brett lowers himself into bean bag.

Brett
Oh, feel the pressure,

Scene 12 Interior – Kath's house *(Good room)* – Day

Kath is reading The Jane Fonda Book about Childbirth. *Kel comes in. He is dressed for a run. Kath guiltily puts the book down.*

> **Kath**
> Oh, thought you were going for a run, doll.
>
> **Kel**
> I am. I'm just going to the toot. Are you finished with that? I –
>
> **Kath**
> Oh, wasn't reading it.
>
> **Kel**
> I need something to read.

Scene 13 Interior – Kath's house *(Outside bathroom door)* – Day

> **Kath**
> Kel doll!

Kath knocks on toilet door.

> **Kath**
> I was wondering if we could factor in some one on one face time tonight.
>
> **Kel**
> I'll be out in a minute, doll.
>
> **Kath**
> Yeah. Maybe just a casual tea? You know, F and Cs down on Bon Beach?
>
> **Kel**
> You're on.
>
> **Kath**
> Alright.

Another Announcement

Scene 14 Interior – Brett and Kim's unit – Day

Kim is sulking.

> **Kim** *(voiceover)*
> Everyone's so self-obsessed. Am I the only person around here thinking about me? The way Mum's carrying on, it's like she's having the baby. Brett's pretending to be pregnant, and now Sharon is going to the Commonwealth Games.

Scene 15 Interior – Hall/Audition room – Day

> **Sharon**
> Aussie, Aussie, Aussie, oi, oi, oi!

Scene 16 Exterior – The beach – Day

Kath and Kel are walking along the jetty.

> **Kel**
> Oh, look at that, Kath. There's the ship's pilot piloting a ship into Port Phillip Heads. Kath?
>
> **Kath**
> Oh, sorry, doll. Million miles away.
>
> **Kel**
> Penny for your thoughts, lovely lady.
>
> **Kath**
> Oh, I don't know, Kel. I'm just really worried about this whole children issue with you. I mean, it's alright for me. I've had a baby. I've had Kim, but ... what about you? You've got zilch. Haven't you ever wanted to have a child?
>
> **Kel**
> It's never been a big deal for me.

Kath
> Really? You don't want to see your genes carried on?

Kel
> Oh, no problem there. I used to be a donator to the sperm bank quite regularly. I mean, who knows? There might be lots of little Kel and Kelly Knights running around out there.

Kath
> What, Kel? A sperm bank?

Kel
> Yeah, used to be a bit of a hobby of mine. You know, something to do.

Kath
> Oh, really? You're joking.

Kel
> No, you know. Doing your bit for society, helping out infertile couples. Haven't done it for years. Is that a problem, Kath?

Kath
> No, heavens.

Scene 17 Exterior – The beach – Day

Kath has a daydream sequence. She sees lots of little children with Kel's hair and ears.

Scene 18 Interior/Exterior – Kim's car/Community centre – Day

Sharon
> Well I suppose, at the end of the day, it's all for the best that my dream didn't come true 'cause now I can come to your birth classes with you.

Kim
> Well I wasn't going to go on my own. What would that look like? Why'd you get kicked out of the volunteers again?

Sharon
> Oh, I'm what's called an enforced voluntary redundancy, which sort of turned out to be a bit of a blessing in disguise, Kim, 'cause I didn't realise. They don't actually pay volunteers.

Kim
> Oh and Sharon, you'll have to double as my bean bag. I had to leave it at home. Brett's glued to it, literally.

Sharon
> Yeah, sure, Kim. No worries. 'Course

Scene 19 Interior – Brett and Kim's unit – Day

Brett is sitting in the bean bag patting Cujo, reading the baby book.

Brett
> It's gotta be here. There it is. Cujo. It means pretty girl. You're a pretty girl, yes you are. You're a pretty girl.

Scene 20 Exterior – The beach – Day

Kath and Kel are sitting in the dunes on a blanket, drinking cups of wine.

Kel
> I was going to tell you, Kath.

Kath
> It's fine, Kel. I'm cool with your sperm donoring. But you know, what about you and me? What about our future?

Kel
> What about it, Kath?

Kath
> Well, I think we both have a lot of love to give.

Kel
> And make.

Kath
> Seriously, though Kel, I mean, we're both rattling around in that great big home. You know, I think it's crunch time. I think it's time we had that talk.

Kel
> I'm all ears.

Kath
> You know, you're a tremendous person, Kel Knight.

Kel
> More Cockfighter's?

Kath
> Yes, please.

Scene 21 Interior – Community Centre – Day

Kim is sitting on Sharon on the floor. She has her legs apart. The instructor is Bettina.

Bettina
> Relax into the beanbag.

Sharon
> Oh, Kim! You're heavy!

Kim
> Bettina, my bean bag is complaining.

Bettina
> All the stress, let it go. Feel your toes and let it go. Breathe and let it go, and any little niggles you might have about the baby or anything, any worries, don't be shy. You can talk here. Let it go.

Sharon
Hi, I'm Sharon. Sharon Strezlecki. I've broken my fibia five times, I have hives and a cold sore. I was recently retrenched as a Commonwealth Games volunteer, and I'm a bit desper-ately ... lonely.

Sharon is crying.

Bettina
Oh, it's alright. Let it go. Let it out. That's a good girl.

Sharon
Oh, thanks, Bettina.

Scene 22 Exterior – The beach – Day

Kel
So, it's decided?

Kath
Oh, it's exciting, isn't it Kel? You don't think we're too old, do you?

Kel
Oh, it'll make us young.

Kath
Oh, they're a lot of work.

Kel
What do you want? A boy or a girl?

Kath
I don't care, as long as it's healthy and attractive.

Kel
If she's anything like you, she'll be beautiful.

Kath
Oh, you great hunk-o'-spunk.

Kel
Come here.

Kath
>Oh, Kel, that feels nice. What do you call that?

Kel
>It's just a banksia cone.

Scene 23 Interior – Kath's house *(Garage)* – Day

Kel's bottles of home brew are sitting fermenting away. All of a sudden they start to pop their crown seals.

Scene 24 Interior – Kath's house *(Kitchen)* – Night

Bottles of beer are overflowing on the kitchen bench.

Scene 25 Interior – Brett and Kim's unit – Night

Brett is at home on the beanbag. The home brew in his stomach is also bubbling away and he too starts popping off. Cujo stands and walks away.

Scene 26 Interior – Kath's house *(Kitchen)* – Day

Kath wipes down bench in kitchen.

Kath
>Oh, pooh, this beer smell. It pongs.

Kim
>You should smell our place.

Brett
>Yeah, it was the dodgy yeast, Mrs. D.

Kath
>Oh, yeast? I've got a book I can lend you on that, Brett. It can be a bugger to get rid of.

Kim
>So what's the story, Mum? Why are we all here?

Kath
> You'll find out when Kel comes back. Now, tell me Kim. How did you go at birth classes?

Kim
> Oh, no, Brett was right. I'm not going back.

Sharon
> Oh, I loved it, Mrs. D. I'm definitely going back. You are looking at an official birth class volunteer.

Kath
> Oh, but Kim, you've gotta go to birth classes. They teach you how to manage labour. You know, your breathing and positions. Whether to crouch on all your fours or your whatnot.

Kim
> Well if it's any of your beeswax, I will be sitting up having a Bailey's and a Pine light.

Kath
> Oh as if, stupid girl.

Kim
> No, I've got full hospital cover. I'm going to have the works. You know, gas, pethidine, epidural. You know, I've paid for it. I may as well use it.

Brett
> Oh yeah, we paid for it, Kim.

Sharon
> Yep, Kim, that's right.

Kim
> That's right.

Kel enters, looking proud.

Kath
> Well alright, peoples. I'm glad you're all here.
> Well, we're glad you're here.

Sharon
> Are you alright, Mrs. D?

Kim
> Yeah, you look weird, Mum.

Kath
> Well I am feeling a bit weird, thank you, Kim. But also, very proud to announce that Kel and I –

Kim
> Oh my God ...

Kel
> ... are going to hear the pitter patter of little feet.

Kim
> Oh, you are joking!

Kath
> Yes, Kel and I have decided to enrich our lives, and we are soon going to be blessed with a beautiful little ...

The dog comes in looking exactly like Kath: a clipped poodle with a big Kath-like hairdo wearing a little brocade waistcoat.

Kel
> And here she is.

Kath
> Isn't she pretty?

Brett
> What breed is it?

Kath
> What is she, Kel? A poodle, shnoodle or a labradoodle?

Kel
> Multidoodle.

Kath
> Multidoodle.

Brett
> She's beautiful. What's her name?

Kath
> Well, Kel and I have come to a joint decision, and we're going to christen her Eponnee Rae.

Sharon

Oh, well. Oh, how about I put on some hotdogs, eh? Oh, sorry, Eponnee.

Kim

Eponnee Rae? That was going to be our name for the baby!

Kath

Shh, Kim, you'll scare her! Eponnee Rae, Eponnee Rae, look at me, look at me. Look at me, Eponnee Rae. I've got one word to say to you, Eponnee Rae. Good girl.

Scene 27 Exterior – Kath's house *(Backyard)* – Day

Kim and Kath sit in garden.

Kim *(on phone)*

Mm? Yeah?

Kath

Anyway, Kim, vis a vie the Eponnee Rae issue. Look, it was sad, but I had to get rid of her. I mean, you know, she tinkled in my good room, pooped in my white boots –

Kim

Shut up, Mum. *(Into phone)* And does that include entrée? Yes, and what wines do you have by the glass? Alright, thank you. No, I'll get back to you. *(To Kath)* Listen up, Mum. Listen to this place. St. Peter's Women's Privates has sushi and a choice of cardonnay or riesling by the glass.

Kath

Oh, hey, hey, hey. St. Peter's. That really sounds like hell. Not.

Kim

Yeah. So, um, what were you saying about Eponnee Rae?

Kath
> Oh, yes. Well, the breeder apparently was desperate to get her back because you know those mushroom shaped top knots, they're quite rare in poodles. So they're going to take Eponnee up to the country to get cloned, I think.

Kim
> Cloned? Cloned on the head. Don't be naïve, Mum!

Kath
> Oh, you're cruel to poor Eponnee Rae.

Kim
> Cruel but fair.

Kath
> Actually, you can have that name back now if you want it.

Kim
> Oh, no, no, don't want it anymore. When I was doing the hospital tour yesterday, I heard some beautiful names. What about Enema for a girl, or Lupus for a guy?

Kath
> Oh, they're nice.

Kim
> Aren't they nice?

Kath
> Yeah, actually, you know when I had my hozzie stay, I heard a beautiful name for a girl. I.V.

Kim
> Oh, that's pretty.

Kath
> Pretty, isn't it?

Kim
> What about Catheter? I thought of that, but I thought it'd be a bit confusing.

Kath
> Catheter. That's nice.

Kim
Yeah.

Kath
Or for a little boy, you could have Neil by Mouth.

Kim
Yeah.

Kath
That's nice, too.

Kim
What about Italian? 'Cause I love Italian names. Cardio. Cardio Infarction.

Kath
Oh, you can't have that? He'll get Farct for short.

The Shower

☆ Kel's mate Sandy comes for a visit
☆ Kath's head is turned
☆ A shower for the baby
☆ The Wrestling comes to Festival Hall

Scene 1   Interior – Kath's house – Day

Sharon is in a chair reading a book.

> **Sharon**
> Oh! Warnie.
>
> **Kath**
> Oh.

Kath has gone to trouble over her appearance.

> **Sharon**
> Oh gee, you look really tizzed up, Mrs. D. Where are you off to?
>
> **Kath**
> Oh, well Kel's mate, Sandy Freckle, is coming up from the beach tonight, Sharon.
>
> **Sharon**
> Oh.
>
> **Kath**
> And we're all off to take in a Leonardo di Caprio double at the Astor.
>
> **Sharon**
> Oh, I am a Leonardo aficionado, Mrs. D. Which ones are you seeing?

Kath
Um, 'The Beach' and 'Who's Eating Gilbert Grape?'.

Sharon
Oh, yeah, no, top films the both of them. Yeah, so who's this Sandy Freckle character?

Kath
Oh, well he's Kel's best mate, but it's funny, I've never met him. Yeah, they had some sort of barney, but they've patched things up and they're all off to the wrestling on Saturday, which is nice.

Kim and Brett enter from upstairs.

Kim
It's fake, Brett!

Brett
It's not fake, Kim.

Kim
It's fake. They're not really fighting.

Brett
So The Rock and The Undertaker are just pretending. Well, that'd be pretty stupid, wouldn't it, Kim.

Kim
They're not the stupid ones, Brett.

Brett
I asked Kel. He used to wrestle when he was in the navy.

Kim
Oh, is that what they called it?

Kath interjects.

Kath
You got a sleeping bag, Brett? The one with the hood?

Brett
Yeah, thanks, Mrs. D.

Kath
What do you need it for?

Brett

I'm going to camp outside Festival Hall tonight, so's I can get ringside seats for the wrestling. WWE: Global Warning.

Kath

Oh, Festival Hall. That takes me back. Oh! 1977, the Leo Sayer concert. Oh, it changed my hair.

Brett

Oh, yeah. I gotta go. See you later, Kim.

Kim

Bye.

Brett

See ya, Mrs. D.

Kath

Yeah, ta ta, Brett.

Brett

See ya, Sharon.

Kath

Okay, girls. Look, while we've got a window, I think we really need to bang our heads together re your baby shower, Kimmy.

Sharon

Oh, righto.

Kath

Okay? Sit down.

Sharon

Oh, this is exciting. Kimmy, you are going to have kittens when you see what I've got for you.

Kim

Oh, I hope not, Sharon, you fool.

Kath

Right. On my list, I've got Aunty Norma. Ah, she's a given. Shona Siddharta, Betty and Bill Cuthbert, Geoff and Gail.

The Shower

Kim
Why do you have to invite them for?

Kath
Because I have to, Kim.

Kim
Well about my friends? Hello!

Sharon
Ah, well Tina rang. She can't come. Ah, no apparently, she has to stay home with a pencil in her eye.

Kim
Oh, well I don't care, as long as she drops off a present.

Sharon
Alrighty. Well, I'd better get on the blower and start inviting.

Kath
Okay. Ooh, I'm gonna have a quick fag. You watch out for Kel, will you? Yeah, then I'd better go and put a bit more face on for that famous Freckle character. I am thinking he might be good for you know who, Kimmy.

Kim
Who?

Kath
Someone over there in the Jason reclinal area.

Sharon *(on the phone)*
Yeah, okay. Alright. Yeah, yeah, no worries. Alright, yeah, I'll tell her. Alright, Simone. Okay. *(To Kim)* That was Simone. She reckons she might be sick on Saturday night, or so she says.

Kim
Oh, well she always says that.

Sharon
So Mrs. D, is Sandy single? You know, is he good looking? What's he like?

The Shower

Kath
> Oh Kel raves about him. I think he's a beach bum. But he used to work in television out at Channel 0 at Nunawading.

Sharon
> TV.

Kath
> Mm.

Sharon
> Wow.

Kath
> Yeah! I think he might be right up your alley, Sharon. Fingers and toes.

Kel enters, nervous.

Kel
> Come on, Kath. He's going to be here in a minute. You'd better get changed.

Kath
> Yes. Oh well, I am changed, Kel. These are my new stovepipes.

Kel
> Oh sorry, love. Could you just do up your top button? I'm a bit toey.

Kath
> Yeah, alright.

The doorbell rings. Kel goes to answer it. Kath puts out her fag and squirts her breath freshener, then gives a little spray as if it is perfume.

Kel
> Oh, that'll be him. Long time no see, stranger! Come on in.

Sandy
> Look at you. You've been grazing in the top paddock mate, haven't you, eh?

The Shower

Kel
> Yeah. Kath, this is Sandy. Sandy, this is Kath.

Kath
> Oh, hello Sandy. Pleased to meet you.

Sandy
> Gidday spunky trunks. Alexander Freckle at your service. Kel, you sly dog. You didn't tell me she was such a looker.

Kath
> Oh thank you, Sandy. I do go to trouble.

Sandy
> You look like trouble to me, hot stuff.

Kath
> Oh! Sandy!

Sharon
> Hello. Sandy, I'm Sharon. Sharon Strezlecki.

Sandy
> Hello.

Kath
> And, um, Sandy, this is um ... This is ...

Kim
> Kim.

Kath
> Kim!

Kim
> My name is Kim.

Kath
> I know. Kimmy, this ... this is Sandy. Sandy, Kim. My daughter.

Sandy
> Kim.

Kel
> Well, we'd better get a wriggle on. The Val Morgan ads wait for no man.

Sandy
> You've still got it, haven't you mate, eh?

Kel
> Come on, Kath.

Kath
> Yes, I'm coming.

Sharon
> I was getting a bit of a vibe, Kim.

Scene 2   Exterior – Festival Hall – Day

Brett is at the head of the queue. He is talking to the guy next to him. The guy wears earpieces and is listening to music.

Brett
> Huge undertaking for The Undertaker Saturday night.

Guy
> Oh, yeah. Yeah, good one. Good one. I bet The Rock smells something cooking. You got your sleeping bag and everything.

Brett
> Oh yeah.

Guy
> Yeah, good one.

Brett
> I'm looking forward to a good night's sleep. My wife's pregnant. She's stacked on about thirty kilos. It's like sleeping with Andre the Giant. The bed's like this.

Guy
> Oh, good one. Good one.

Brett
> And she kicks. Oh, you got no idea.

Guy
  No, I don't have any idea.

Brett
  Anyway, I'm going to sleep like a baby, I can feel it.

Guy
  Oh, good one. Yeah.

Brett
  What are you ... listening to there?

Guy
  Oh, Dire Straits.

Brett
  I love Mark Knopfler. He's a genius. Genius.

Guy
  He is a genius.

Brett
  I know.

Guy
  Would you like to have a listen?

Brett
  Cool. Thanks, mate. What have we got? What have we got? Oh, the sultan.

They dance together and the guy tries to get past.

Brett
  Hey. Hey, hey, hey, mate, come on.

Guy
  What?

Brett
  No, there was a queue. There was a queue.

Guy
  I thought we were just dancing together. I mean, not in a ... I don't ...

The Shower

Brett
> It's alright.

Guy
> 'Cause they're the sultans of swing, and ...

Brett
> I know they are. Just ... just leave it at that, alright? It's cool. Just don't do it again, alright?

Guy
> I didn't even do it in the first place. I ...

Brett
> Just ...

Brett gets out his thermos.

Brett
> Braised steak and vegies.

Scene 3   Interior – Kath's house *(Good room)* – Night

Kel, Sandy and Kath are sitting in the good room. Sandy and Kath are laughing.

Kel
> Yeah.

Kath
> Oh snap, Sandy. That is exactly my feeling about tonight. You know, the parking, the seats, the cup holders.

Sandy
> Oh my word, yes.

Kath
> Yes, it was a nice night.

Sandy
> Indeed. Magic.

Kath
> Alright, drinks?

The Shower

Kel
> I'll have a Kahlua.

Kath
> Oh, I meant Sandy, Kel.

Sandy
> Oh well, I think I feel like a, ah ...

Kath and Sandy
> A brandy crusta!

Sandy
> Oh dear Kath, you must be psychic.

Kath
> Oh, they're just my favourite too, Sandy. Assaulted nut?

Kath offers him the bowl. They touch hands. They have a moment. Kath goes to the kitchen.

Kath
> I'll just get the drinks.

Sandy
> Tell me, Kel. What's the story with the two fat ladies in the kitchen?

Scene 4   Interior – Kath's house *(Kitchen)* – Night

Sharon and Kim are talking. Sharon is going over the RSVP list for the baby shower.

Sharon
> So who have I got? Danielle, Rachelle, Rochelle and Michelle.

Kim
> Oh, good.

Sharon
> ...can't come.

Kim
> Oh, stuff 'em. Never liked 'em anyway.

Kath
Oh, excuse me, Kim. I'm looking for the brandy balloons.

Kim
Oh, keep your wig on. What are you on? Stop singing!

Kath
What? What are you talking about?

Kim
Mum, you're breathing funny!

Kath
What? No I'm not.

Sharon
That Sandy's very nice, isn't he Mrs. D?

Kath
What, Sharon? Oh, I hadn't noticed.

Kim
I reckon he's a bit of a sleazebag.

Kath
No, Kim. Don't cast nasturtiums on Sandy. He's Kel's best mate.

Kim
Well if he's his best mate, why wasn't he at the wedding?

Kath
Well I don't know. They had some issues back then. Something about a Japanee lass. Anyway, it's none of your or my beeswax, alright? Hey, stop drinking out of the bottle. That's disgusting. Go and get a tumbler, please.

Scene 5   Exterior – Festival Hall – Night

Everyone is asleep in the queue. Brett and Guy are leaning on each other. Brett just has the sleeping bag on, but not pulled up. You don't really see it.

The Shower

Scene 6   Interior – Kath's house *(Good room)* – Night

Sandy
Thanks mate for seeing me. But you know, Kel, I ... I was hurting too, big time. And if I could turn back time, I would. But you know, Kel, hindsight's a wonderful word.

Kel
No, mate, it's me that should be thanking you.

Sandy
Hmm?

Kel
If you hadn't done what you did, I wouldn't be here with that foxy lady in the kitchen.

Sandy
Yeah. And she is a fox, mate. A real fox. You lucky dog.

Kel
Any word from ... Yoko?

Sandy
Hmm? Oh yeah, Yoko, yeah. No. No, no, no, no. No, she shot through, mate. She took me to the cleaners. Disappeared off the face of the earth. I guess you could say, Kel, women and me, we don't mix.

Kath enters and gives Sandy his drink.

Kath
One brandy crusta.

Sandy
Thanks, princess.

The Shower

Scene 7   Exterior – Festival Hall – Day

Brett is lying alone on the pavement asleep. He is in Kath's sleeping bag with the hood on. It is really girlie – blue with white stars and pink fur trim. Brett wakes up, and can't get out of the bag. His thermos is in front of him, empty. He has been duped.

Brett
   What? oh, no! Hey mate! Oh no! No, no, no!

Brett wriggles around in sleeping bag.

Brett
   Stupid bloody zip! Oh God.

He bounces over to the box office and the ticket seller.

Brett
   Hey, can I have three tickets, please!

Scene 8   Interior – Fountain Gate Mall (Maternity shop) – Day

Kim and Sharon are shopping in a maternity shop. Kim comes out in a funny maternity outfit, holding up a pair of huge maternity undies in skin-tone, and a bra.

Kim
   Yes, I will take this. And can you tell me, do these come in a G string? Oh, and I need a triple H cup for this. But look, this one's broken. I didn't do it. I'll just have a look around. What else do I need?

Sharon
   So ... so Kimmy, do you really reckon that Sandy likes me?

Kim
   Yep, definitely.

Sharon
   But he completely ignored me the whole time and was chatting up your Mum.

Kim
> Sharon, that's the oldest trick in the book. You know, the ricochet flirt. The more they ignore you, the more they like you.

Sharon
> Gee, you must have heaps of guys who like you.

Kim
> They're only human. Nuh, I like this better. What do you think, Sharon?

Sharon
> I think I'd really like a great big stuffed avocado. Can we go to the food court, Kim?

Scene 9 Interior – Fountain Gate Mall (Food court) – Day

Kim and Sharon are in the food court, standing in queue.

Sharon
> I don't know. Maybe I'll have a Mexican with double cheese. What are you going to have, Kim?

Kim
> I don't know. Something light. Maybe a skinny latte and skinny cheesecake with double skinny cream.

Sharon
> Hey Kim, isn't that your Mum over there?

Kath and Sandy are at a table looking at the menus. They look intimate.

Sandy
> Well I'll tell you something, Kath. That Thai chicken pie, it's got my name on it.

Kath
> Yeah, I can't decide, Sandy, between the panini, the puccia or the ham and cheese pinyata.

Sandy
> The pinyata. Mmm.

The Shower

Kath
Oh, I ... I think I'll just go for the croissant thanks, Sandy.

Sandy
The croissant it is, then.

Kim and Sharon come over to Kath and Sandy's table.

Kath
Ooh, hello Kim.

Kim
Mum, what are you doing here?

Kath
Sharon. You know Kel's mate, Sandy.

Sharon
Hi, Sandy.

Sandy
I'll just get into line, hot stuff.

Kath
Okay, Sandy.

Sharon
How are you today, Sandy? Enjoying Melbourne?

Sandy completely ignores Sharon.

Kim
I thought you said you were too busy to come to Fountain Gate today.

Kath
Yes, well, no. No, well, you know, Sandy rang just after you two left, and said he'd like someone to come and show him Melbourne's hot spots. So ... here we are.

Kim
Alright. I'll see you at home.

Sandy comes back with food.

Sandy
Hey, beautiful. Your croissant. Do you want it filled?

Kath
Thank you, Sandy. That'd be ... nice. Thanks.

Sandy
My pleasure.

Sharon
I think you're right, Kim. I think he really likes me.

Kim
Told you.

Scene 10 Exterior – Kath's car/Nepean Highway 'Sights' – Day

Kath is driving her car. Kath and Sandy are taking in the sights of Melbourne. They are really boring sights. They are flirting.

Kath
You see, Sandy? There's Ikea, and they've extended that right back. Then a bit further back you've got Barbecues Galore ...

Sandy
Mm.

Kath
Which is nice.

Sandy
Yes.

Kath
And then you've got Cartridge World, for all your cartridge needs, etcetera, etcetera, etcetera.

Sandy
Etcetera.

Kath
Yeah, and then this is the golden mile, with Rey Hunt Motors, you've got your Lexus, you got ah, Fords, Honda.

Sandy
Oh!

The Shower

Kath
It's all here in Melbourne. It's marvellous, Melbourne.

Sandy
Yes, indeed it is. Yeah, you like to get around, don't you? You are a bit of a goer, aren't you Kath? Yeah, you are a bit spunky, aren't you? Yes, you are a bit spunky in your ...

Kath
Oh, stop it, Sandy! Don't do that.

Sandy
Beep beep Barina.

Kath
Stop it, Sandy. I'll run off the road.

Sandy
Let me ... blow your horn.

Kath
Stop! Stop that. You're so naughty.

Scene 11 Interior – Kath's house (kitchen) – Day

Sharon is blowing up balloons. Kim is doing her nails.

Sharon
You know, with my aerobic capacity, Kim, I could blow up about fifty balloons with one breath. It's because I've got big lungs. Wonder if Sandy likes big lungs.

Kim
Right, that table's just for the presents. Oh, has Tina dropped 'round my present yet?

Sharon
Oh no, not yet, Kimmy. Actually, speaking of presents. Do you want to see mine now?

Kim
Oh, yeah, yeah! Gimme, gimme, gimme!

The Shower

Sharon
> Close your eyes. I haven't had time to wrap it yet.

Kim
> A teething ring?

Sharon
> Yeah. It's for the baby.

Kim
> Oh, der fred. Eighty nine cents at Coles. Is that all I'm worth to you? Eighty nine bloody cents at Coles?

Kim throws down ring.

Sharon
> Oh, Kim. The baby can't count. It won't know it's cheap.

Kim
> I can't believe you're so mean, Sharon. Right, that's it. You can't be godmother. No, sorry Sharon. The baby's not going to be around mean people.

Sharon
> Oh no, Kimmy, please. It was just a joke. It was just a joke.

Kim
> Well I'm not laughing, and I've got a very good sense of 'umour!

Sharon
> Oh, I'm sorry, Kim. I've got you another present.

Kim
> What?

Sharon
> Well, you remember how I told you I had to give up my beloved golf because I had carpal tunnel?

Kim
> What's that got to be with the price of Tia Maria?

Sharon
>Well, it wasn't quite true. Um, I sold my golfclubs and my membership so I could buy you this. I got you the biggest one, Kimmy, so you could get in there, too.

Sharon starts to cry.

Kim
>That's quite nice. I just ... lost my sense of 'umour with your stupid jokes. Do you want a tissue?

Sharon
>Yeah, that'd be nice, thanks.

Kim
>They're in the kitchen. Your godmother status is still up in the air.

Scene 12 Exterior – Motel carpark/Kath's car – Day

Kath and Sandy are in Kath's car. They are in the carpark at The Buckingham Motel, where Sandy is staying.

Kath
>Oh, you're a hoot, Sandy.

Sandy
>Mm.

Kath
>No, it was a really tremendous day. I mean that.

Sandy
>Oh, it's been magic.

Kath
>Yeah.

Sandy
>Oh well, yeah. Kath, that's my hotel room there.

Kath
>Oh, just there? That's handy.

The Shower

Sandy
> Yes, it's, ah, it's cold and lonely, Kath. Just me, the television and a spa.

Sandy moves across to kiss Kath.

Kath
> Nuh. I'd better go, Sandy.

Sandy
> Yes.

Kath starts the car and backs out. Her hands-free mobile starts ringing.

Kath
> Hello? Kel?

Scene 13 Interior – Kath's house *(Kitchen)* – Day

Kel
> Just driving around on your own, are you? Oh, I see. You're a funny old thing, aren't you? Yeah, alright. Okay, I miss you. Okay, bye.

Kel is unloading the dishwasher from the night before. He gets out the two brandy balloons. He studies them and looks slightly concerned.

Scene 14 Exterior – Street/Kath's car – Day

Kath is driving.

Kath *(voiceover)*
> Get a grip, Kathleen Day-Knight. What are you doing? Yes, Sandy Freckle is a very attractive man, but what's Kel? He's a great hunk-o'-spunk, that's what, and a tremendous person to boot. Oh, but Sandy has a way. Oh, Sandy, Sandy, Sandy. I can't get you out of my head. Oh! There's Officeworks. I might just zip in there and get some nice coloured card. Yeah, make a sign for Kim's party.

The Shower

Scene 15   Interior – Kath's house (kitchen) – Day

Sharon is sitting around the kitchen getting ready for the shower tea.

> **Kath**
> Oh Sharon, microwave those pastizzis first, otherwise they'll take yonks.
>
> **Sharon**
> I'm on the case, Mrs. D.
>
> **Kath**
> Now, what have I gotta do? Cracker-wise, what have I got? I've got your Jatz, your Ritz, your Clix.
>
> **Sharon**
> What about your Savoys, Mrs. D?
>
> **Kath**
> Oh no, they'd just confuse people, Sharon.

Scene 16   Exterior – Kath's house – Day

> **Kel**
> Yeah, it's a Daewoo, and the gold's quite rare, actually.
>
> **Sandy**
> Yeah? Well, you are doing well, aren't you Kel?
>
> **Kath**
> Okay, that's done. Oh, hello Kel. Hi, Sandy.

Awkwardness between Sandy and Kath. Sandy ignores Kath and focusses instead on Sharon.

> **Sandy**
> Gidday, it's Sharon, isn't it?
>
> **Sharon**
> Yeah.
>
> **Sandy**
> And isn't that the Sapphires?

The Shower

Kath and Sandy are guiltily ignoring each other.

Kel
> You, ah, you alright, sweets?

Kath
> Oh yes, Kel. I'm just a bit busy, actually.

Sandy
> Are you the captain, are you? Gee, that's, ah, that's great.

Sharon
> Yeah. So, um, will we be seeing you tonight at Kim's baby shower?

Kel
> Oh no, Sharon. We're going to the wrestling. Let's get ready to rumble! Oh look Sharon, he's got me in the half nelson!

Kel and Sandy start to play wrestling.

Sandy
> Oh, ahh!

Kel
> Oh, stop crying, you girl. I'm lethal.

Sandy
> Good old Kel.

Kel
> Ah, where's my man bag? Ah, there.

Kath
> Kim! Kimmy, are you ready? She's so excited. She's making herself look beautiful.

Kim comes in to the kitchen.

Sharon
> Oh my God, Kim!

Kim
> What?

The Shower

Kath
> Oh Jesus H. Gilbert Grape.

Kel
> Two pounds of licorice allsorts, thanks.

Kim
> What?

Kel
> You look like the Darrell Lea girl.

Kim
> I do not. No one else would think that.

Brett comes in the back door.

Brett
> Hi, Kim. Oh, I'll have some bullets and some rocky road, thanks.

Kim
> Oh, you can all get stuffed, the pair of yis.

Brett
> Oh, what'd I say?

Kel
> Come on, Brett. Let's get going before we put both our feet in it.

Brett
> Yeah. See ya, Shas. See ya, Mrs. D.

Kel
> See ya later, sweetie.

Brett
> See ya, Kimmy.

Kath
> See ya later, Kel. Bye, Sandy.

Sandy
> See ya, Captain. Sapphires, Sapphires ...

Sharon and Sandy
> ... don't put us down!

Sharon
Yeah. Yeah.

Kel, Brett and Sandy exit.

Sharon
Nuh, he hates my guts, Kimmy. Yeah, me and Sandy, over before we even began.

Kim
How do you know?

Sharon
Well, um, he kept talking to me, and he was really nice. Yeah, it was a real ricochet flirt if ever I saw one, Kim. He must really like you, Kimmy.

Kim
What's not to like?

Scene 17   Interior – Kath's house (Good room) – Night

The baby shower is in full swing with Aunty Norma and couple of others, and one girl with a crying baby. (We don't see the baby.) Kim is opening the presents.

Mona
Brionney's really advanced. She's got a huge IQ.

Kim *(sotto voce)*
Lucky. She's bloody ugly.

Mona
You are gonna love that.

Kim
What is it?

Mona
Kim, it is a baby monitor. You can take that and hear the baby crying wherever you are, whatever you're doing. You'll always hear that crying.

Kim
What else is there?

The Shower

Mona
: Because Brionney's gifted, we're having her extended. She's just crying 'cause she's really bored here.

Kim
: She's bored!

Scene 18   Interior – Kath's house (kitchen) – Night

Guilty Kath is nervously cooking pineapple fritters. Kim enters.

Kim
: Bloody Mona and her baby whiney Brionney are really getting up my goat. I mean, it's a baby shower. Why did she have to bring her baby?

Kath turns to reveal she has a black face.

Kath
: Here, Kim. You can take those out. They're ready.

Kim
: Mum, they're burnt!

Kath
: Oh, just say they're Cajun style, Kim. Have I got something on my face?

Kim
: Nuh.

Scene 19   Interior – Kath's house (Good room) – Night

Later in the evening the baby shower is still on. Kel, Brett and Sandy return. Kel and Brett go into the good room. There is lot of baby stuff, including the playpen all set up.

Kel
: Gidday, girls. Getting up to no good? How did my sausages go down?

Brett
: So, it's all still happening. Good baby shower?

Kim
Whole lot of people sitting around talking about babies. Whoo hoo!

Scene 20 Interior – Kath's house (kitchen) – Night

Sandy approaches Kath in the kitchen.

Sandy
Kath, are you ignoring me?

Kath
Oh, no Sandy. Can I get you something?

Sandy starts getting a bit fresh. Kath gets away.

Kath
Don't, Sandy.

Kath leaves the kitchen and goes down the hall. Sandy follows Kath down the hall. Kel sees them go.

Kel
Just excuse me.

Scene 21 Interior – Kath's house *(Hall/bathroom)* – Night

Kel appears in the hall, and sees Sandy follow Kath into the bathroom. Sandy shuts the door. Kel follows them and opens the door. Kel confronts Sandy.

Kel
What the hell is going on here?

Sandy
Oh, mate. Nothing. Absolutely nothing. Not a thing.

Kel
You bastard!

Sandy
Oh dear.

The Shower

Kath
> No, Kel. I can explain!

Kel
> No, I'll explain. You want to know why I've been left at the altar four times?

Sandy
> Oh, here we go.

Kel
> You're lookin' right at him. You're not a freckle. You're a moll.

Sandy
> Come on, mate. Calm down. That's ancient history.

They move from the hall into the good room where all the presents and the guests are.

Kel
> Every fiancee I've ever had, this worm'd muscle in on.

Sandy
> Well mate, why not? They were begging for it.

Kel
> But for once, I used my noggin and I married you first. He wasn't going to get you then, and he's not going to get you now.

Sandy
> Too late, mate. Been there, done that.

Kath
> No, Kel. It's not true. It was just a silly frisson over a croissant at Fountain Gate. Nothing really happened.

Sandy
> Yeah, 'cause I stopped it.

Kath
> Oh no, Kel. It's not true.

Sandy
> Well mate, who are going to believe?

Kel
> Right, Freckle.

Kel puts Sandy in a headlock. The fight is on. They are grappling and scuffling. They fall in to the playpen.

Kath
> Oh, no! Kel! Oh no, stop it! Stop it!

Brett
> Get out of there, Kel. Get out of it. Nice move.

Kath
> No, leave him alone, Kel. You're too strong for him!

Brett
> Come on, Kel. Come on. Get him in.

Kath
> It's all my fault!

Brett
> Come on! Cage match! Cage match! Get out of there, Kel. Don't let him put the sleeper on! He's not ... oh no, that'll kill him, mate. He's getting him in the sausage maker.

Kel
> Do you give in? Do you give in?

Brett looks knowingly at Kim.

Brett
> Not real eh, Kim?

Scene 22 Interior – Kath's house (kitchen) – Night

Later that night, Kath and Kel are in the kitchen.

Kath
> I don't know what happened back there, Kel. Sandy turned my head and it was screwed on backwards for a minute. I'm sorry, doll.

Kel
> Oh, it's not your fault. Sandy Freckle is irresistible. Even I can see that. He's got the look.

Kath
> No, Kel Knight, you've got the look. Come here, you.

Brett
> Nah, he's gone mate. He's running off down Whitehorse Crescent like a stunned chicken. You kicked his arse, Kel. You did good, mate.

Kel
> Could have been a contender, you know. Killer Karl Kel had a pretty nice ring to it.

Brett
> Hey Kel, Smack Down, Channel 8.

Kel
> No, don't worry about.

Kath
> No Kel, you watch it. We can wrestle later.

Brett
> Thanks, Mrs. D.

Scene 23 Interior – Kath's house (Good room) – Night

The guests have gone. Sharon and Kim are looking at the presents.

Sharon
> What's this, Kimmy? A horn for the baby's pram?

Kim
> No, it's a breast pump.

Kath
> Oh, you've done well, Kim.

Sharon
> Gee, that ... that Sandy turned out to be a bit of snake, didn't he?

The Shower

Kath
> Yeah, and I think we're talking trouser, Sharon, but don't go there, girlfriend. Oh, look at this. Oh, look Kim. It's a Hi-5 jolly jumper. Isn't that beautiful. Beautiful pressies.

Kim
> Yeah, all for the baby, none for me!

Kath
> What's this one?

Kim
> Oh, that's Tina's present. She's got a great sense of 'umour. It's gas for the birth. Will I give it a go?

Kath
> Yeah, give it a go. Good fun.

Kim puts on the mask and has a suck. When she speaks her voice is squeaky from the helium.

Kim
> Oh, that's nice. It's different. It's unusual!

Kath
> Oh, give us a go, Kim.

Kim
> Yeah, nice. Nice. Oh! Oh! My waters have broken!

Kath grabs the mask.

Kath
> Kimmy! Kimmy!

Kim
> Ahh!

Kath
> Look at me! Look at me! Look at me! Look at me! Now I got one word to say to you, Kim. Pant, pant, blow!

Kim
> Ahh! Ahh!

The Shower

Sharon
>Don't panic. Don't panic!

Kath
>It's alright, Kimmy. It's alright Kimmy!

Kim
>Mum! Ow! Ow!

Kath
>I'll ring the phone. I'll ring the phone! I'll ring the phone!

Kim
>Oh, wait! It's gone.

Kim screams with Sharon and Kath

Kim, Sharon and Kath
>Ahh!

Scene 24 Exterior – Ambulance – Night

Kim is wheeled out on a gurney and loaded into ambulance. Kath gets in as well.

Kath
>You'll be right. That's a big crack there. Thank you, Peter.

Kim
>Where's Brett?

Kath
>Watch out for the Commodore.

Kim
>Where's Brett?

Kath
>Oh Kimmy, you don't need Brett. You know Brett can't stand the sight of you ...

Kim
>What?

Kath
... in pain. No, he'll come later when Smack Down's finished. I'll get in, and I'll be here holding your hand.

Kim
Oww! Hold my hand, Mum.

Kath
I can't with those nails.

Kim
Oh, Mum!

Kath
You'll be right. Shh!

Scene 25 Exterior – Street/Ambulance – Night

Kim is screaming.

Kim
Oww!

Kath
Oh pipe down, Kim. Driver? Driver, look, there's no need to rush. No, don't go ... I wouldn't go this way. Take the more scenic route. Go up through Wattletree Road. It's very nice that way. Takes a bit longer, but you get to see the elms. It's shocking what they've done to them. They've chopped the middle out to accommodate the power lines, which is very sad for the Wattletree Road residents, I feel. Have you been driving long? I had to take an amblance recently when I had my papilloma removed. And, um, I just wanted to ask, 'cauoc I had a very nice driver. An Egyptian fellow. I think his name was Amar. He was very good looking ...

Kim
Oh, shut up!

Kath
... and I don't know what happened to him. Kim, just having a conversation, with Barry up here, and he's being very patient with you.

Kim
Oh, hold my hand! Hold my hand!

Kath
You're not the first girl in the world to have a baby now pipe down. You've got hours, Kim. Hours and hours.

The Hideous Truth

* The past revisited
* Kim's baby is born
* An unexpected person returns

Scene 1   Interior – The Hospital   Day

Kim is in hospital. We hear a baby crying in background. Nurse enters carrying flowers.

> **Nurse**
> These are for you, Kim.
>
> **Kim**
> I'm finding it hard to cope, Sister. She's crying all the time, and she's very windy.

Cut to Sharon crying in corner.

> **Nurse**
> Oh, right. Well, I'll take her for a while. Come on, Sharon. That's it. Let's go.

Sharon does a big burp as Sister pats her back and leads her out.

> **Sharon**
> Oh, sorry. It's just that hospitals really make me cry, which is hard given that I work in them all the time.

Kath bursts in.

> **Kath**
> Don't panic, don't panic. I'm here. So what have they said, Kim?

Kim
> Right, they said it was a false alarm, but they want me to stay in 'cause I don't look so good.

Kath
> Oh, well that's boring. We could be here till the crack of sparrows.

Kim
> I know. I'm so over it, Mum. I'm having second thoughts about this baby.

Kath
> Well, it's a bit late now, Kim. This is a very bad hospital corner. I think you'll find you'll be having second, third and fourth thoughts before your time's out.

Kim
> Mum, leave it. Oh, where's Brett? Why isn't he here?

Kath
> Brett doesn't need to be here, Kim. He's got to be at the new Maribyrnong store today. He's got his grand opening.

Kim
> Well, his grand opening? What about my grand opening?

Kath
> Oh don't be foul, Kim. I'd better go move the Barina. I'm parked in the ambliance bay. I won't be long. Stay there.

Kath exits. Sharon comes back in.

Sharon
> Don't worry, Kim. I feel heaps better now.

She burps again.

Scene 2   Interior – The Hospital – Day

Sharon, Kath and Kim are sitting waiting. Kath has her water crackers and some dips and sports bottles of water.

Kath
>Sharon, have some humus with a water cracker. It's very nice.

Kim
>Did I tell you Mum, Brett bought me a ring?

Kath
>Oh, did he, Kimmy? That's beautiful. Is it from the Diamond Company?

Kim
>No, a rubber ring, for after the birth, for my business end.

Kath
>Oh, well I'll tell you Kim, if your birth's anything like the one I had with you, your business end'll be closed down for renovations for quite some time.

Kim
>Oh, it's not fair. It's never going to come. Get out!

Kath
>I hate to tell you, I was two weeks late with you. Oh, you had no intention of going anywhere. You just sat in there like a stunned mullet. Nothing's changed.

Kim
>Oh, shut up, Mum!

Kath
>I remember it like yesterday. I was huge. It was a terrible summer.

Dissolve to flashback:

Scene 3 Exterior – Pool showroom/office (1973) – Day

Kath pregnant in 1973. She has a seventies perm growing-out, parted in the middle, and wears funny 70's maternity clothes. Gary Poole (Kim's dad) is there. There are a man and woman next to Gary at edge of pool.

Gary
... to Molly Meldrum. Story there, but I won't go into it now. Hey, Kath! Can you come and get the creepy crawly out of the kidney shape?

Kath
Alright, Gary. There's a phone call for you.
I think it's Honkers.

Gary
Gary's Pools, Gary Poole speaking. Nuh. No, you are. As if. Der fred. Righto Wendy. Ta ta. Hey, ah, Kath, get on the blower to TAA and Cathay. I've got to get to Honkers toot sweet.

Kath
What, now, Gary?

Gary
Yeah, those slippery dips, the fibreglass ones we ordered. They've gone missing at customs.

Kath
But Gary, the baby, it's due any day now.
I'm already overdue.

Gary
Baby, the baby. That baby is going to be the bain marie of my life.

Gary grabs a chocolate bar.

Kath
Oh Gary, don't have another Polly Waffle. Cholesterol!

Gary
Give it a bone, Kath! How about an Escort?

Kath hands him a cigarette.

The Hideous Truth

Kath
Oh, donkey root? Yes, I read somewhere, Gary, that the more I smoke, the smaller the baby'll be and I'll get my figure back quicker.

Gary
Yeah, well, hope you're right. It's not good for business you lookin' like that.

Kath
Oh, yeah, I know, Gary. My hair. But I try and go to trouble. It's just I haven't been to Fay for my midweek comb up. I'll just Busy Girl it.

Kath gets a can of Busy-Girl and sprays it in her hair. Gary is back on the phone.

Kath
Is that better, Gary?

Gary
Shhh! Yeah, Renae. Listen, yeah, buy up big in Poseidon. Yeah, it's gonna be 'uge. Yeah, and send the rest to the Cocos Islands. No, don't worry about the house. That's in Kath's name. They can't touch it. Okey dokey.

Kath
What was that, Gary?

Gary
You know your beeswax, Kath? Why don't you mind it? Well, come on, Kath! It's not bush week. My clothes aren't just gonna pack themselves, you know.

Gary walks out of the office. Kath grabs her stomach as if she is going into labour.

Kath
Alright, Gary. Gary? Gary!

Gary
Yeah, yeah.

Scene 4   Interior – The Hospital – Day

> **Kath**
> Oh, and the rest, as they say, is 'istory, Kim.
>
> **Kim**
> So Dad had the smarts. That's where I get it from. I take after him.
>
> **Kath**
> Oh no you don't, Kim. Gary was a fat, lazy whinger who was terribly rude.

Kim's mobile rings.

> **Kim**
> It's Brett. Hi. No, nothing's happening, no thanks to you.
>
> **Kath**
> Kim! Turn your mobile off!
>
> **Kim**
> How long? Half an hour?

She points to the signs.

> **Kath**
> Kim!
>
> **Kim**
> *(To Kath)* Mum, it's for emergencies! *(Into mobile)* Can you get me a bottle of Coke? Two litre. Alright, bye.
>
> **Kath**
> Poor Brett. He's so gorgeous.
>
> **Kim**
> What are you crying for now, Sharon?
>
> **Sharon**
> Oh, you're just so lucky, Kim. I'm so happy for you. A spunk rat husband, a renovation and soon, a baby. I just wish I had a little bit of what you've got, Kim.

Kath
> Oh, Sharon. You've always been very unlucky in love, haven't you? Never had anyone special?

Sharon
> There was someone, once.

Dissolve to flashback:

Scene 5   Interior – Kath's old house (1984) – Day

Kath's old house in 1984. Kath has a helmet perm and is dressed like Lady Di. Kim has love bites all over her neck. Music is playing. Sharon is in the downstairs bathroom, fixing her hair.

Kath
> Oh, I like this one. What's this called?

Kim
> 'Uman League.

Kath
> Oh, 'Uman League. Oh, it's trendy, isn't it? Now, where are my Saint Moritz?

Kim
> Oh, you're always losing them. Don't look at me.

Kath
> Well don't look at me.

Kim
> Well don't look at me!

Kath
> Kimmy. Kimmy. Don't look at me, please. Don't look at me. Now turn that down please, Kim. Dallas is on. It's the Kerry Armstrong episode tonight.

Kim
> Sharon! Have you done my homework yet? Sharon!

Sharon
> Hi, Kim.

Sharon enters, dressed in a blitz outfit with perm - short on sides.

Kim
What's your story?

Sharon
I'm going out tonight, Kim. I've got a date.

Kim
What, a date? With a guy?

Sharon
Yep. We're going to a blue light disco at Necropohiliac's. It's going to be a Blitz night. *(Sings)* Ahh, Vienna.

Kim
Well, who is this so called guy?

Sharon
Oh, he goes to the tech. And Kim, he drives.

Kim
What, a car?

Sharon
Yep, Datsun Bluebird. I really think he likes me, Kimmy. You know, we've got so much in common. He loves indoor cricket.

Kim
Oh, super daggy.

Sharon
And, we're both born on the same day and ... he thinks I'm a really great blitz dancer.

Kim
Oh, as if, Sharon! Great blitz dancer. Anyway, I'm not hanging around. I'm going for a smoke.

Sharon
Oh no Kimmy, please stay! Please stay and meet him. He's really ace. You'll really like him. Oh please, please, please, please –

Kim
> Sharon! Shane would be spewing blood if I even looked at another guy.

Kim goes upstairs. The doorbell rings. We hear Kath.

Kath
> I'll get it! Oh, hello. *(Whispers)* Spunky. Very spunky.

Sharon
> Oh, hi Brettie.

Brett
> Hi, Sharon.

Sharon
> You look great.

Brett
> You look ace.

Sharon
> Um, oh, Mrs. D, Brett. Brett, Mrs. D.

Brett
> Hi, Mrs. D.

Kath
> Hi, Brett. Call me Kathleen, won't you?

Brett
> Kathleen.

Kath
> I've got to go. I'm watching Dallas.

Brett
> Oh, grouse.

Brett walks over to Sharon and they kiss. Kim enters and walks between them.

Kim
> Excuse I. Just gotta get my Limmits.

Sharon
> Oh, Kimmy, this is Brett. Brett, Kimmy.

Brett is mesmerised.

Brett
> Hi, Kim.

Kim
> Hi, Brett. Would you like a Passiona?

Sharon
> Oh, no, no, Kimmy. Brett doesn't like soft drinks. Anyway, Brettie, we've gotta go.

Brett
> I love Passiona.

Kim
> Oh, could you come and help me here? This cupboard's really high.

Brett
> Oh, I'd love to help.

Kim
> You're tall, aren't you?

Brett
> Yeah, six two.

Kim
> Wow. You know, if there's one thing I love, it's Passiona –

Sharon
> We ... we gotta go, Brett. Ready? Brett! Brettie!

Dissolve back to present:

Kim *(out of Sharon's mouth)*
> Brett! Brett!

Scene 6   Interior – The Hospital – Day

Sharon is crying at the memory. Kim and Kath are oblivious. Kim is on the phone.

Kim
Brett. Brett, you're a dickhead.

Sharon
I need a Passiona.

Sharon exits.

Kim *(To Kath)*
He's locked his keys in the car.

Kath
Ohh!

Kim *(To Brett on phone)*
Well, how long's that going to take you, stupid?

Kath
Oh Kimmy, I'll go and get him. I'll take the car and go and get him.

Kim
Listen up. Mum is going to come and pick you up. Wait out the front. Do you think you can do that? Alright.

Kel
Any movement at the station?

Kath
Oh, no, Kel. But we're in crisis mode here. Brett's stuck over in Maribyrnong at work. We've gotta go and get him,

Kel
Oh! I'm double parked out the front. I'll drive.

Kath
Kel, it's Maribyrnong Plaza, for God's sake! It's tricky over there! Five different entrances. No, I know it like the back of my hand. Give me the keys. I'll drive.

Kel
>The Daewoo's a manual, love. Maybe I should drive.

Kath
>No, Kel, don't be absurd. I'll be alright. You navigate. Can you read a Melway's?

Kim makes another phone call.

Kim
>Yes. Could I have a club sandwich, some fries, a glass of riesling, and what inhouse movies do you have? Oh, same to you. Stupid.

Sharon enters with a can of Solo she is sniffing annoyingly.

Sharon
>They don't have Passiona so I had to get a Solo instead.

Kim
>Could you stop sniffling?

Sharon
>Oh, sorry Kim.

Scene 7   Interior – Little Town Hall – Day

Back to 1984. The town hall is tizzed up like a blue-light disco. Sharon and Brett are blitz dancing to Misex's 'Computer Games'.

Sharon
>I work part-time in this new takeaway food shop. It's called McDonalds. Yeah, I got ninety nine cents an hour, which you know, is fine. I'm s'posed to get a dollar six, but you can eat all the chips you want.

Brett
>Does Kim work there?

Sharon
>No, Kim doesn't work. This is grouse.

Brett
> Oh, yeah. Yeah, Kim's grouse.

Sharon
> Oh, Brettie, I'm so rapt in you. I'm really stoked. Today is the first day of the rest of my life, and it's gonna be ace keen.

Kim enters, dressed as a suburban version of Madonna. She is back-lit so she looks like a vision. The song is 'Total Eclipse of the Heart'.

Kim
> Hi.

Brett
> Jeez, you're a spunk.

Kim
> That's what everyone says.

Brett is captivated by her unnatural beauty.

Brett
> Do you want to go round with me?

Kim
> I'll have to drop Shane. Yeah, okay.

Brett
> Ace. I'll get us a drink.

Sharon
> Kim, what are you doing? Brett's my boyfriend! Brett! Brettie, I'll have a drink! I'll have a drink, Brettie! Kim, Brett's s'posed to be rapt in me, not you!

Kim
> Sharon, I can't help it if he's captivated by my unnatural beauty!

Scene 8   Interior – The Hospital – Day

'Unnatural Beauty' resonates repeatedly back to the present day Unnatural beauty ... unnatural beauty ...

> **Kim**
> I'm hungry. Feel like something healthy.
>
> **Sharon**
> What about some fruit, Kimmy?
>
> **Kim**
> Oh, good idea. Can you get me a Cherry Ripe?
>
> **Sharon**
> Sure.
>
> **Kim**
> Jumbo size.
>
> **Sharon**
> Yeah, sure.

Scene 9   Exterior – Freeway/Kel's Daewoo – Day

Kath is driving.

> **Kath**
> I think I'll take the, ah, Werribee turnoff onto the ring road, then zip up through Footscray, Kel. What do you say? Kel?
>
> **Kel**
> Oh, sorry sweets. I was, ah, a million miles away. Can you believe it? This is only the second time I've let a lady drive my car.
>
> **Kath**
> Really?
>
> **Kel**
> Mm.

Kath
>Oh, I feel honoured. *(She grates the gears.)*
>Ooh. Sorry, Kel.

Kel
>Yeah, you're the first since 1977.

Dissolve to flashback:

Scene 10   Exterior – Shopping centre carpark/Kel's old car (1977) – Day

1977. The first time Kel was jilted. Kel's car is being driven by a matronly woman, Sheila.

Kel
>No Sheila, you're still riding the clutch. Just let it all the way in. So, that's settled. The reception's at The Cuckoo. Very pricey, though.

Sheila drives into a shopping centre car park and parks the car.

Sheila
>Kelvin, I have some good news and some bad news. The good news is, I have won Tattslotto.

Kel
>Whoo hoo! Forget The Cuckoo! Travelodge, here we come!

Sheila
>And the bad news is, I am in love with Sandy Freckle and I'm leaving you. Coming, Sandy!

We see Sandy in a Channel O car nearby. Sheila hops in and they drive away.

Dissolve to present:

Scene 11   Interior – Kel's Daewoo – Day

Back in the present, Kath is driving Kel to Maribyrnong.

Kath
>Yeah, he was a bad egg, that Sandy Freckle.

Kel
> And that was just the beginning. It was all downhill from there.

Dissolve to flashback:

Scene 12 Exterior – The Beach (1974) – Day

The second time Kel was jilted. It is 1984 and Debbie and Kel are watching the surfing.

Kel
> Someone's surfing out there.

Debbie
> Yeah.

Kel
> Isn't that great?

Debbie
> I know.

Sandy comes up with his board.

Sandy
> Gidday, gidday, gidday.

Kel
> Sandy Freckle! I didn't know you were back from overseas.

Sandy
> And who might this be? You're not the Big M girl, are you? You've got more front than Myers.

Kel
> This is my fiancee, Debbie. We're getting married next week.

Sandy
> Kel, your lilo. Your lilo's being blown away by the wind.

Kel runs after the lilo. He comes back and Debbie and Sandy are rolling around in the sand.

Dissolve to another flashback:

Scene 13 Interior – Fountain Gate Mall (1990) – Day

The third time. 1990. Kel and a Drag Queen are coming down the escalators.

> **Kel**
> So, do you like the ring, princess?
>
> **Drag Queen**
> Oh, it's ... it's beautiful. But Kelvin, there's something I've been meaning to tell you. I thought you would have cottoned on by now. I can't keep living this lie. I want to have Sandy's baby.

Sandy is waiting at the bottom of the escalator.

> **Sandy**
> Sorry Kel, mate, but this one's for real.
>
> **Kel**
> Jan! Jan!

Dissolve to another flashback:

Scene 14 Interior – Bridal Hire Shop (2000) – Day

The fourth time. Kel is returning the wedding suit (the powder blue with the velvet piping).

> **Mark**
> Oh, hello Mr. Knight. Everything set for tomorrow?
>
> **Kel**
> The wedding's off.
>
> **Mark**
> Again? What, didn't the Japanese lass like you in the powder blue? I thought you looked stunning in it myself. What would I know? Only been in the business twenty years.
>
> **Kel**
> *(Starts crying)* I'll go.

Mark
(Uncomfortable) Yes, perhaps that would be for the best.

Kel leaves the shop. Mark calls out to the dressing room

Mark
Mr. Freckle! You're in luck. The powder blue is available.

Sandy
Gee, that's, er, that's great.

Back to present:

Scene 15 Interior – Kel's Daewoo – Day

Parking the car at Computacity, Kel is gazing at Kath.

Kath
What are you staring at, Kel Knight?

Kel
Oh, just the foxiest lady this side of Fountain Lakes, that's all.

Kath
Well, I reckon your four former fiancees were the biggest pack of nongs to let you go.

Kel
Oh, I've been to hell and back to get you, Kath Knight.

Kath
I'm not easy, Kel.

Kel
No, but you're easy on the eye.

Kath
Oh, ditto, you great hunk-o'-spunk.

Kel
Yeah. We're like peas in a pod like that, aren't we?

Brett comes out of Computacity

Kath
Oh, there's Brett.

Kel
Oh. Now, Brett and Kim. Now there's a perfect match.

Kath
I remember their first date. They went to the footy.

Dissolve to flashback:

Scene 16 Exterior – Football/ Brett's car – Day

Kim and Brett are on there first date, sitting in Brett's Bluebird watching a VFL match.

Brett
Go for the bounce, son! Go, Hawks! Go, the Hawks! Yeah, I'm gonna go round the whole world. You know, Europe, India, Bali. Yeah, the whole lot. Nothin's gonna tie me down. I was really stoked you agreed to come today. You smell nice. Are you wearing Tweed?

Kim
Nuh, Charlie.

Brett
I love chicken Twisties, don't you?

Kim
Nuh.

Brett
Do you like the Hunters? Hunters and Collectors?

Kim
As if.

Brett
This is going really well. I've got a really good feeling about us. Jeez, you're a spunk. Can I give you a love bite?

Kim
Yes.

Kim pulls her hair away from her neck.

Scene 17   Interior – The Hospital – Day

Kim and Sharon are playing cards on the bed.

> **Kim**
> Well have you got a nine?
>
> **Sharon**
> Go fish. Have you got an eight?

Suddenly Kim goes into labour.

> **Kim**
> Oh! Sharon!
>
> **Sharon**
> Kim, are you alright?

Sharon dithers.

> **Sharon**
> Don't worry, Kim. I'll ... I'll go and get someone, alright? Don't worry. Everything'll be okay. Alright?

Sharon turns around, looking for a nurse. When her back is turned, Kim cheats with the cards.

> **Sharon**
> Just ... just –

Kim drops the act.

> **Kim**
> Ha ha. Sucked in.
>
> **Sharon**
> That is not funny, Kim.
>
> **Kim**
> Yes it is.
>
> **Sharon**
> You cheated.

The Hideous Truth

Kim
> Any obs?

Sharon
> I'm not listening to you anymore, Kim.

Sharon sits, puts in her earset and listens to sport. Kim feels something.

Kim
> Oh! Oh, Sharon! Sharon!

Sharon
> I can't hear you!

Kim
> No, I'm not joking, Sharon.

Sharon
> La la la la ...

Kim
> It really hurts.

Kim
> Sister!

Sharon
> La la la la!

Kim
> Sharon!

Kim
> Sister! Ow!

Nurse
> Okay, dear. It's okay.

She's going into labour.

Kim
> It hurts!

Nurse
> What kind of a friend are you? Going to the delivery room. Can you walk to the delivery room? Just put your legs over.

The Hideous Truth

Scene 18 Exterior – Kel's Daewoo – Day

Brett, Kath and Kel are in the Hyundai chatting, oblivious to Kim.

> **Kel**
> There's a Red Rooster up there, Kath.
>
> **Kath**
> Oh, I can't get across four lanes, Kel. KFC's coming up, I think. Do you like that?
>
> **Kel**
> Mmm. What do I feel like?
>
> **Kath**
> Yeah, I don't know. I feel like something light, actually. Maybe a salad.
>
> **Brett**
> It's green Kath. You know, go.
>
> **Kath**
> Oh, don't panic, Brett. She hadn't even had a niggle when we left.

Scene 19 Interior – The Hospital – Day

Kim is in labour. Sharon is comforting her.

> **Sharon**
> Oh, Kimmy, just try and relax, Kim. Just breathe into it, Kim. Just try and ... try ... Kimmy, it's beautiful, you know. It's what God made us for, Kimmy. It's beautiful. It's natural.
>
> **Kim**
> It hurts!

Sharon moves down to other end of bed.

> **Sharon**
> It's alright, Kimmy. Sharon'll have a look. Sharon'll have a look. Okay? Oh, it's hideous! It's unnatural! God's a bastard! Aghh!

Sharon runs from room screaming.

> **Kim**
> Give me a Caesar!

Scene 20 Exterior – Kel's Daewoo/Drive thru – Day

Kel, Kath and Brett are in the drive thru.

> **Kath**
> I'll have the Caesar.
>
> **Brett**
> Make mine a Greek salad.
>
> **Kath**
> Anything for you, Brett?
>
> **Brett**
> No.
>
> **Kath**
> Oh, this takes me back.
>
> **Kath**
> Kim was born over there.
>
> **Brett**
> What, in 7-11?
>
> **Kath**
> Oh, you're a scream, Brett. No, it used to be the Mater Misery Hospital.

Dissolve to flashback:

Scene 21 Interior – Mater Misery Hospital (1973) – Day

Kath in 1973 holding a baby who is all small and quiet and lovely.

> **Kath**
> I'm going to call her Kimberly Dianne Poole. So small. So quiet. Looks just like me.

Nurse comes in holding a big fat baby with lots of black hair and squawking.

Nurse
Sorry, Mrs. Poole. Bit of a mix up. Here's your baby.

Nurse leaves with the other 'lovely' baby.

Kath
Oh. But I liked ... but I like that one.

Baby cries. Gary comes in smoking.

Gary
Kath?

Kath
Oh, here she is, Gary.

Gary
Oh, fat little grunter.

Kath
Oh, that's just baby fat, Gary. She'll lose that.

Gary
Plain as an arrowroot biscuit. Anyhoo, I'm off to Honkers.

Kath
What, now?

Gary splashes on some aftershave – Brut 33.

Gary
Yeah, yeah, got a plane to catch. Any chance of a bit of shoosho? Pick you up a carton of fags.

Kath
Alright, Gary. Bye bye.

Gary
Yeah, yeah.

Scene 22 Exterior – Road/Kel's Daewoo – Day

Back in the present, Kath, Kel, and Brett are in the car, eating and chatting.

Kath
And that's the last we saw of Kim's Dad. Him and Wendy Patterson, our pool model, disappeared into a tax haven somewhere.

Kel
What a low life.

Kath
Oh no, Kel. It was a blessing in disguise. I got the house, which I sold for a bomb in the boom.

Kel
And that's when you and Kim moved to Fountain Lakes?

Kath
Yeah, and I've been living high with the hog ever since.

The mobile rings and Brett answers. He goes suddenly pale.

Brett
Brett Craig? Oh my God. Kim's in labour. Quick, let's go. Thanks, Shaz.

Kath
Oh, she'll be hours, Brett.

Kath grinds the gears again.

Kath
Sorry, Kel.

Scene 23 Interior – The Hospital – Day

Kim is asleep in bed. Sharon is trying to wake her.

Sharon
Kim! Kimmy! Kimmy, wake up, Kimmy! You've had a baby.

Kim wakes up.

Kim
    Where's my flute of bubbly?

Sharon
    Ooh.

Kim
    Oh, that didn't hurt at all. I don't know what women go on about.

Sharon
    Well, Kimmy, I mean, you did have a general anaesthetic.

Kim
    Well that's hardly the point, Sharon.

Kath, Brett and Kel burst in.

Brett
    Are you alright?

Kath
    Oh, Kim!

Brett
    And the baby?

Sharon
    A little girl, Brettie.

Brett
    Oh, Kimmy!

Brett goes to give Kim a hug.

Kim
    Hey, get off my drip, Brett!

Brett
    Oh sorry, sorry, sorry.

Kath
    Clever girl!

Kel
    Congratulations, Brett.

Brett
>Oh, thanks Kel. Thanks mate.

Kath
>Oh, so Kimmy, is she beautiful?

Kim
>I don't know. I haven't seen her yet. I was completely out to it. Another flute of bubbly, please.

Sharon
>Oh, sure Kim.

The Nurse enters with the baby.

Nurse
>And here she is.

All
>Ooh!

Everyone has a look and reels back in horror. The baby is black. Kim has a flashback: Imran!

Scene 24 Interior – Restaurant/New Year's Eve (9 months ago) – Night

Drunk Kim on the prowl. She is looking for Imran, and finds him.

Kim
>Imran. Happy New Year! Imran! Imran.

Back to the present.

Scene 25 Interior – The Hospital – Day

Kim is looking confused and guilty. Everyone is looking shocked. Another nurse bustles in.

Nurse
Oh my giddy aunt! You've got baby Kahn!

All
Ohh!

Kath
Ohh!

Nurse
Here's your Eponnee!

Kath
Oh, she looks just like you, Brett.

Brett
Hello, Eponnee.

Kath
Oh, give us a hold, Kim.

Kim
No! Gee, she's heavy. Do they make infant Lite'n'Easy?

Kath
Oh Kimmy, leave off about her weight.

Sharon pours them a drink.

Sharon
And Mrs. D.

Kath
Thank you. Fill me up.

Sharon
Ah, ah, Kel, Savoury Shape?

Kath

Alright. I want to propose a toast. Kimmy, Brett, Sharon, Kel. Eponnee Rae. Eponnee Rae? Look at me, please. Look at me. Look at me, Eponnee Rae. Oh, I think she's got a wandering eye, Kim.

Kim

Mum!

Kath

Okay, let's have a toast, peoples. To Eponnee Rae, darling, may you have a long and preposterous life.

All

To Eponnee's preposterous life!

Kath

I feel tiddly already.

Kim

Oh, thank God I can drink again.

Scene 26 Interior – The Hospital – Day

Kim is propped up in bed drinking. Kath is there.

Kim

Mm, this riesling's going down nice.

Kath

Yes, Kim, I think in the end, St. Peter's Women's Privates was a good choice.

Kim

Yeah.

Kath

It's ve– ... can you smell that?

The current-day Gary Poole enters. He has lost a lot of hair.

Kath

That's Brut 33. I hate that.

Gary
   Gidday, pussycat.

Kath
   Oh, I think you got the wrong room.

Gary
   I don't think so. Here's your fags, Kath.

Kath
   Gary?

Kim
   Dad! Dad, it's Kim. Your little princess.

Gary
   Still as plain as an arrowroot biscuit. Well, more like a Weston's Wagon Wheel, actually.

Kath
   Gary, what are you doing here? What ... what happened to Honkers and your business and everything?

Gary
   Down the gurgler. I'm skint. How was I to know that Hong Kong was going to be invaded by the Chinese?

Kath
   Oh.

Gary
   Anyhoo, what's news Mrs. Poole?

Kath
   Oh, no, Gary. I'm Mrs. Knight now.

Gary
   I don't think so. I never signed the divorce papers.

Kath faints.

Kim
   Mum? Mum, look at me! Look at me!
   Look at me! I've got one word to say to you.